# Man in Conflict

## Traditions in Social and Political Thought

# DICKENSON BOOKS OF RELATED INTEREST

# Man in Conflict

## Traditions in Social and Political Thought

*Louis I. Katzner*

*Bowling Green State University*

**Dickenson Publishing Company, Inc.**

*Encino, California and Belmont, California*

ISBN: 0-8221-0165-3
Library of Congress Catalog Card Number: 75-7294

Printed in the United States of America
Printing (last digit): 9 8 7 6 5 4 3 2 1

Cover design by Preston J. Mitchell

*To my mother, a woman of valour,*

*and my father, a man of great insight*

# Contents

# The Dickenson Series in Philosophy

Philosophy, said Aristotle, begins in wonder—wonder at the phenomenon of self-awareness, wonder at the infinitude of time, wonder that there should be anything at all. Wonder in turn gives rise to a kind of natural puzzlement: How can mind and body interact? How is it possible that there can be free will in a world governed by natural laws? How can moral judgments be shown to be true?

Philosophical perplexity about such things is a familiar and unavoidable phenomenon. College students who have experienced it and taken it seriously are, in a way, philosophers already, well before they come in contact with the theories and arguments of specialists. The good philosophy teacher, therefore, will not present his subject as some esoteric discipline unrelated to ordinary interests. Instead he will appeal directly to the concerns that already agitate the student, the same concerns that agitated Socrates and his companions and serious thinkers ever since.

It is impossible to be a good teacher of philosophy, however, without being a genuine philosopher oneself. Authors in the Dickenson Series in Philosophy are no exception to this rule. In many cases their textbooks are original studies of problems and systems of philosophy, with their own views boldly expressed and defended with argument. Their books are at once contributions to philosophy itself and models of original thinking to emulate and criticize.

That equally competent philosophers often disagree with one another is a fact to be exploited, not concealed. Dickenson anthologies bring together essays by authors of widely differing outlook. This diversity is compounded by juxta-position, wherever possible, of classical essays with leading contemporary materials. The student who is shopping for a world outlook of his own has a large and representative selection to choose among, and the chronological arrangements, as well as the editor's introduction, can often give him a sense of historical development. Some Dickenson anthologies treat a single group of interconnected problems. Others are broader, dealing with a whole branch of philosophy, or representative problems from various branches of philosophy. In both types of collections, essays with opposed views on precisely the same questions are included to illustrate the argumentative give and take which is the lifeblood of philosophy.

*Joel Feinberg*
*Series Editor*

# Preface

The emotionalism and violence of the late 1960s and early 1970s are apparently a thing of the past, the abuses of Watergate now a part of the public record, and the United States is preparing to celebrate its bicentennial year. We may well be entering a period in which there is a genuine desire to confront the most fundamental issues of politics and society on a rational basis. How much authority should governments have and how much autonomy should individuals have? What is the best form of government? Why should people live under the authority of others in the first place? Is individual freedom possible and, if so, how important is it? What is the just way of distributing wealth among the members of society? As the shouting dies down, it is again possible to hear these questions crying out for answers.

However, *Man in Conflict* has not been written to provide *the* answer to these questions. First and foremost, it has been written as an introduction to help clarify, bring to life, and put into focus the basic philosophical issues of politics and society. Second, it attempts to give insight into the various positions that can be taken on these issues. Consequently, I have tried to keep my own views—which would probably be described as either liberal or bourgeois depending upon your point of view—entirely out of the picture. However, there can be no doubt that the book is at least tinged by my liberal leanings. And finally, in *Man in Conflict* I hope to convey some of the excitement and joy that can come from raising basic philosophical issues of politics and society and thinking about them in a critical way.

The book lends itself to a variety of uses. Because it is a genuine introduction, presupposing neither background in philosophy nor familiarity with the issues, it can be used in introductory courses either as the main text or in support of readings in primary sources. Second, because the discussion of specific socio-political systems (communism, fascism, and democracy) is reserved for the final chapter, and the earlier chapters deal with the central concepts of social and political thought (freedom, authority, justice, sovereignty, rights, etc.), the book can be used in courses which focus either upon communism, fascism, and democracy or on central concepts. And finally, it can also be used as collateral reading to provide important background and perspective in courses dealing with specific issues in social and political thought—for example, philosophy of law, philosophy of the state, philosophy of punishment, distributive justice, and so on.

Many teachers, colleagues, family, and friends have contributed to the final product in numerous ways—some that I am aware of and more that I am not. However, a few individuals have made singularly direct and important contributions. Hence I would like to acknowledge,

Joel Feinberg, Donald Scherer, and numerous anonymous reviewers—
for their critical and helpful comments on earlier drafts
of the manuscript.

Janet Greenblatt and Marianne Polachek—
for their expert editorial assistance.

Pat Bressler, Bonnie Kathrens, and Joyce Stephens—
for their excellent typing.

And Linda, Kelly, Sylvia, Jamey, and Jody—
for their love.

*Louis I. Katzner*

# Man in Conflict

## Traditions in Social and Political Thought

# 1

## The Underlying Concepts

The purpose of this book is to introduce you to some of the more significant issues of social and political philosophy. The first question to consider in such an endeavor is, What is the nature of the philosopher's concern with social and political issues? In an attempt to answer this question I begin by considering what philosophy is all about, and then discuss how philosophical concerns about social and political issues differ from other kinds of concerns with these issues.

### WHAT IS PHILOSOPHY?

This question is itself an important philosophical issue. Moreover, as with all philosophical issues, there are a number of different ways to answer it. The significance of this fact for our purposes is as follows: each conception of philosophy emphasizes different issues and deals with those issues in different ways. Hence it is important for you to have some idea of my philosophical orientation in order to see the ideas in the light I intended.

One way of giving an account of the nature of philosophy is to look to the origin of the word *philosophy*; it comes from the Greek word *philosophia*, which means "the love of wisdom." But such information, at least by itself, is singularly unhelpful. In order to know what philosophy is all about, one must see the kinds of ideas philosophers are concerned with and the ways they go about dealing with them. An excellent account of the nature of philosophy has been presented by Elizabeth and Monroe Beardsley, and what follows draws heavily from their work.[1]

The basic concern of philosophy is to discover reasonable beliefs—that is, beliefs that can be supported by reasons. But clearly this does not take us very far, for all intellectual investigation has this goal. The scientist offers a hypothesis which he attempts to support by reasons or evidence. The art critic presents an assessment which he attempts to justify with reasons. Even a football coach attempts to justify the moves he makes with reasons. Hence it is not enough to point out that the basic concern of philosophy is to discover reasonable beliefs; some indication must also be given of how philosophical beliefs differ from other beliefs.

### *Philosophical Questions Are General, Fundamental*

The essential features of philosophical beliefs are best seen by looking at the two basic characteristics of the questions philosophers ask. First, they tend to be general; that is, they probe into broader areas than do questions of other disciplines. Compare the question "Is everyone obligated to obey the law?" with "Is John obligated to pay his taxes?" The former is a question about people and the law in general, while the latter is about a particular person and a particular law. In a like way, questions about the nature of government are more general than those about a particular government. Questions about man's basic nature (if there is such a thing) are more general than those about the nature of a given individual. And so on.

Second, philosophical questions tend to be more fundamental than others—that is, logically they must be answered before the others. For example, the scientist is concerned with discovering all sorts of facts about the world, and he uses an approach (the **scientific method**[2]) which he assumes yields correct results. A philosopher of science, on the other hand, may well ask: Does the scientific method yield correct results? This concern is more fundamental than the scientist's because if the scientific method does not necessarily yield correct results, then all the results attained by using it are suspect. Similarly, to question whether a given form of government is desirable is more fundamental than to ask whether that form of government should be implemented. For, presumably, we should only live under those forms of government that are desirable.

To say that philosophical questions are more fundamental than (or logically prior to) other questions does not mean that people cannot deal with the other questions without first answering the philosophical ones. It is obvious that people do this all the time. Many scientists engage in scientific research without questioning the adequacy of the scientific method and many people claim that a given form of government should be implemented without really considering the desirability of that form of government. Rather, it is simply to point out that whenever this is done, answers to the more fundamental questions are being presupposed; even though the majority of people may not examine the adequacy of these presuppositions, such examination is one of the main tasks of philosophy.

Notice that this description of philosophical questions is vague. It does not indicate how general or fundamental a question must be in order for it to be philosophical. Nor does it rule out the possiblity that there are other characteristics which render questions philosophical as well. All we have said is that philosophical questions tend to be more general and more fundamental than others.

This vagueness is intentional, not an oversight. To be any more precise would require a degree of thoroughness and complexity out of place in a work of this kind. The important point is that the discussions that follow involve more general and more fundamental issues than you normally concern yourself with.

## The Method of Philosophical Investigation

But it is not enough to say that philosophical issues tend to be more general and fundamental. Some discussion of the method of investigation is also needed. The scientist uses the scientific method (**empirical investigation**), to answer the questions he is concerned with. But the more general and fundamental the questions are, the less likely that they can be answered in this way. Hence, empirical investigation is not the fundamental tool of the philosopher.

Basically, the philosopher uses the tool of analysis, which takes two main forms: the analysis of the concepts themselves and the analysis of the relationships that exist among concepts. In order to see what is involved in both these aspects, let us examine the process in a particular case. In *State and Revolution* Lenin says, "Freedom in capitalist society always remains just about the same as it was in the ancient Greek republics: freedom for the slave owners."[3] Yet other thinkers insist that capitalism affords all of its members the largest amount of freedom possible. Thus, for example, Friedrich Hayek claims that "the system of private property is the most important guaranty of freedom, not only for those who own property, but scarcely less for those who do not. It is only because the control of the means of production is divided among many people acting independently that nobody has complete control over us, that we as individuals can decide what to do with ourselves."[4]

Conceptual analysis reveals that Lenin and Hayek attach decidedly different meanings to the word *freedom*. For Hayek, freedom means to buy and sell in the marketplace as one chooses. Moreover, as long as there are no constraints imposed on this freedom by the government (and perhaps by monopolies), then even if one does not have the wherewithal to exercise this freedom, one is free.

For Lenin, on the other hand, to be free involves more than simply living in a formal structure that allows one to buy and sell as one chooses. Without the wherewithal for buying and selling, "freedom" is formal, empty, and meaningless. People are really free only when they have the means necessary for the exercise of freedom (i.e. when they know that freedom exists effectively as well as formally). It is Lenin's assessment that in capitalism the material conditions necessary for the exercise of freedom are available only to the very rich, and that the vast majority of people are enslaved by their poverty.

Thus conceptual analysis reveals that the two claims which initially seemed contradictory are not really so. Given what each side means by freedom, both can be true. The disagreement of course does not end here, but we see it in a new light. The dispute between these two **species** of communism and capitalism is not, as both sides often claim, a struggle between the forces of freedom and the forces of slavery. Rather, the issue is, Which sense of "freedom" is most important, Lenin's or Hayek's?

Having been brought to this realization by conceptual analysis, one is now, if one cares to proceed further, in need of a different form of analysis.

At this point one must determine whether either concept of freedom has unreasonable presuppositions or unacceptable implications. For example, does Lenin's sense of freedom presuppose that human beings do something (such as work without the profit incentive that, because of their nature, they are incapable of doing? Then it is impossible to be free in that sense of the term. Or does Hayek's sense imply or result in a state of affairs that is unacceptable (such as all wealth in the hands of a few families while everyone else is in abject poverty)? Then it would have to be rejected as well. Of course, in the process of tracing the implications and presuppositions of one concept, it is often necessary to analyze and trace the presuppositions and implications of other concepts. In short, the two kinds of analysis—of concepts and of their relationships—although logically distinct, are constantly interacting in philosophical investigation.

The philosophical process is often referred to as **dialectical**, that is, it presents and evaluates reasons both for and against our beliefs. Its goal is to discover which of our more general and fundamental beliefs can best be supported by reasons. To determine this, we give attention not only to the reasons that support a belief but also to those against it. Once we have decided what can legitimately be said both for and against a belief, we then assess the cumulative weight of these reasons in order to make a judgment as to whether the belief should be accepted or not. This dynamic process obviously involves much give and take.

### Benefits of Philosophical Investigation

There are several benefits of philosophical investigation. First of all, conceptual analysis, by examining basic concepts in our beliefs, makes those beliefs clearer. Very often we use concepts such as freedom, authority, justice, etc., without having a very precise idea of what they mean. Analyzing such concepts provides us with both a clearer idea of what they mean and a better understanding of our beliefs about them. As we have seen, analyzing the concept of freedom enables us both to see more clearly what the word means and to have a better understanding of our beliefs about freedom (i.e. how important it is, how free our society is, and so on).

A second benefit of philosophical investigation is that it enables us to hold reasonable beliefs—that is, beliefs supported by reasons. As we put our ideas to the test of philosophical analysis we discover the reasons both for and against those beliefs. And as we examine and evaluate these reasons, retaining those beliefs which have the weight of the reasons behind them and rejecting those that have the weight of the reasons against them, we discover those beliefs it is most reasonable to hold.

Finally, by looking at the relationship between our beliefs, we are able to eliminate the inconsistencies in them. We may find, for example, that our beliefs about freedom lead to conclusions that are incompatible with the existence of government. In this case we would have to either accept the idea that there should be no government, or else modify our beliefs about freedom and government so that they are no longer incompatible with each other; otherwise our position would be inconsistent.

## WHAT IS SOCIAL AND POLITICAL PHILOSOPHY?

Everyone is familiar with the basic social and political concepts—freedom, authority, law, justice, welfare, government, society, and the state. For our purposes it is not necessary to determine which are most properly called social and which political nor to compile a complete list of them. Instead, we focus on the nature of the philosopher's concern with these concepts. Probably the best way to discover about the rather unfamiliar concerns of the philosopher is to find out how his concerns differ from those of scientists in general and social scientists in particular.

The social sciences deal with man as a social being and include political science, sociology, psychology, etc. The term "social *science*" suggests that these disciplines at least claim to be sciences. Basically, when we call a discipline a science, we assert that it uses the method of science (i.e. empirical investigation). Thus it can be inferred that the social scientist believes that human behavior can be investigated empirically in much the same way that the human body or the movement of the stars can be studied. His main concern is to observe, describe, and categorize human behavior. The philosopher, on the other hand, using the method of philosophical analysis rather than the method of empirical investigation, focuses on the concepts used to describe human behavior rather than the behavior itself. His goal is to analyze these basic concepts and the relationships that exist among them, rather than to record, describe, and categorize behavior that can be empirically observed or tested.

### Philosophy Is Normative, Science Descriptive

The word *science* in "social science" also suggests a second important difference between the focuses of social science and of philosophy. A claim scientists often make is that their discipline is value neutral; what they mean is that scientists do not make value judgments. They stick to an examination of "the facts." Whether or not this claim is actually correct (for example, value judgments may be built into the scientific method) is an interesting and complicated issue, but not one that can be pursued here. Important for our purposes is that philosophers unabashedly recognize that problems of value fall within their purview. Because questions of value play an important role in social and political philosophy, it is imperative to distinguish carefully between science and philosophy on this score.

In social and political philosophy it is not enough merely to analyze the basic concepts. The purpose of this analysis is to establish the norms or standards by which we can determine why a particular system, institution, law, or belief is better than another. At the heart of social and political philosophy lie questions such as, What is the best form of government? Which sense of freedom is it most important to pursue? How essential is it that justice be done?

Social science, on the other hand, is **descriptive** rather than **normative**. It is concerned with portraying how things are rather than how they should be (normative). Thus a political scientist may study how people vote in a given election, but not how they *ought* to vote. A sociologist may investigate how free people think they are, but not how free they *ought* to be. A psychologist can attempt to inquire into the most fundamental characteristics of human behavior but not, at least as a scientist, to ask what these characteristics *ought* to be.

The political scientist studies how different political systems function. When our political system is not functioning effectively, we call on him to diagnose the ailment and work out a cure. If we want to know whether a given political system can work effectively, we ask a political scientist to study the matter. In short, the political scientist is concerned with the workability of political systems.

The normative concerns of the political philosopher, on the other hand, lead him in a different direction. He sets out to discover the best or most desirable political arrangement. In the abstract, this simply involves determining which of all the logically possible alternatives is the most desirable. On the practical level, it involves assessing these alternatives on the basis of how workable they are. In many cases the most desirable alternative is probably not workable and the most workable alternative is clearly undesirable. Desirability and workability, then, are independent variables.

Some philosophers concern themselves with assessing the desirability of various alternatives totally in the abstract—that is, without giving any attention at all to the question of workability. For such thinkers, the normative concerns of philosophy are totally independent of the descriptive concerns of the scientist. Other philosophers, however, are not content with the abstract normative judgments that such an approach produces. They are concerned with assessing various alternatives in terms of their workability as well. Thus in deciding which alternative is preferable, they consider both the abstract normative judgment of desirability and the practical scientific judgment of workability. Such people usually find that they must choose between two alternatives, one of which is somewhat more workable, yet somewhat less desirable, than the other.

The difference between these two philosophical approaches lies in what each takes to be the appropriate grounds for judgment. In the former view, the judgments are abstract or based upon philosophical considerations alone. In the second view they are practical, relying upon both the conceptual insights of the philosopher and the empirical data collected by the scientist.

Although both these views accept the ideas that social and political philosophy is basically a normative enterprise and that normative issues are different in kind from scientific or descriptive ones, these ideas are not accepted by all philosophers. In fact, they come under intense attack from a variety of different quarters. To provide some insight into the nature of this dispute as well as to further clarify the distinction between normative and descriptive concerns, it will be helpful to examine two such attacks.

### Naturalism

One attack comes from naturalists, so named because they believe that all normative statements can be reduced to descriptions of the natural world. In other words, once the proper way of translating normative statements into descriptive statements is arrived at, the question "What ought . . .?" becomes a species of the question "What is . . . ?"

One of the best examples of this view is the dictum Might makes right. This statement establishes a naturalistic relationship between questions of right (normative questions) and questions of might or power (descriptive questions). To claim that Might makes right is to insist that there is a very easy way to find out what is right—just look at those in power and observe what they are doing. Then of course what is right becomes empirically observable. If two people disagree about what is right, the dispute is resolved when one of them overpowers the other. There is no criterion by which we can judge as wrong the actions of those with the strength to act. The fact that they have the power to act is what makes the things they do right.

Might makes right is just one of many naturalistic relationships. The important point is that, if one accepts naturalism in any of its forms, the normative issues of philosophy, rather than having their own method of investigation, are resolved in the same way that scientific issues are. Once normative issues are tied to descriptive issues in a naturalistic way (e.g., by the dictum Might makes right) empirical investigation is the appropriate method of inquiry, and the normative issues of social and political philosophy become identical with some of the descriptive issues of social science.

The great advantage of naturalism is that it reduces seemingly insoluble normative issues to matters that can be handled by the tools of the scientist. No longer need people haggle endlessly over whether or not $X$ is the best form of government. Once a naturalistic relationship is accepted the question can be settled permanently, because that relationship makes it possible to demonstrate empirically the correctness or incorrectness of every answer given.

But what happens if one rejects naturalism? What happens if one does not think that normative questions are reducible to empirical ones in the way proposed by the naturalist? What happens if one agrees with those thinkers who insist that, given any proposed naturalistic relationship, a normative question can always be asked, namely, Is what is claimed to be right really right? In other words, given the dictum Might makes right, one can still look at any action taken by those in power and meaningfully ask, I know that they have the power to do it, but is it really right?

### Normative Skepticism

Some thinkers take the view that, if normative questions cannot be answered empirically, they cannot be answered at all. When such a person rejects naturalism, the only alternative open to him is normative skepticism—the view that normative questions simply cannot be answered.

At its weakest, the skeptic believes that although normative questions do have answers, it is impossible for anyone to know what they are. At its strongest, the skeptic holds that normative questions are insoluble because they are meaningless. This latter form is based upon the belief that any statement not empirically verifiable is meaningless.

We see then that, for decidedly different reasons, both the naturalist and the skeptic reject the claim that social and political philosophy is basically a normative enterprise. The former insists that normative issues are merely disguised descriptive ones, while the latter insists that since normative issues are impossible to solve, one must content oneself with exploring descriptive matters.

Furthermore, the dialectic—which leads from the rejection of naturalism to the adoption of skepticism—brings to the fore the most important elements in the claim that social and political philosophy is basically normative. This claim commits one to the position that, although normative issues cannot be resolved by empirical investigation, they are nevertheless important, and should be considered. In other words, it commits one both to the nonempirical nature and to the worthiness of investigating normative issues.

Let's make this point in a somewhat different way. Because we have been raised in a scientific age, it is not surprising that we embrace the scientific method. But we also tend to do something else: we accept the degree of certainty that appears possible in scientific investigation as the degree necessary for being able to say that we know something. Consequently, any enterprise that yields a level of certainty less than that seemingly afforded by the scientific method seems to us an enterprise in which "everything is simply a matter of opinion."

### Are Normative Issues Worth Investigating?

There is a middle ground between these two extremes, which denies that normative issues can be reduced to scientific ones, yet at the same time maintains that normative issues are more than mere matters of opinion. Some opinions are better than others, and it is possible to show this. Hence there is real value in engaging in normative deliberations, the denial of the skeptic notwithstanding.

To a considerable extent, this point is obvious. We have already seen how philosophical analysis leads to the clarification of one's beliefs. We have also seen how it shows us when certain beliefs either entail or contradict other beliefs. If a given position involves a contradiction, then it must be rejected, no matter who holds it. If a given position entails certain beliefs, then accepting the position requires accepting those beliefs; any view which fails to do this must be rejected.

More important, those beliefs supported by reasons should be accepted over those that either have no reasons or have only bad reasons to support them. Notice that I merely have said, "supported by reasons." The point is that even though one may not be able to give reasons that carry the empirical certainty of science in support of normative claims, nevertheless reasons can be given for these claims. And it is possible to inquire as to which beliefs can be supported by the best reasons. This process is precisely what we use next, as we turn to social and political issues.

### NOTES

1. Elizabeth L. Beardsley and Monroe C. Beardsley, *Invitation to Philosophical Thinking* (New York: Harcourt Brace Jovanovich, 1972), pp. 1-11.
2. Terms appearing boldfaced can be found in the Glossary.
3. V. I. Lenin, *State and Revolution* (New York: International Publishers, 1932), p. 72.
4. Friedrich A. Hayek, *The Road to Serfdom* (Illinois: University of Chicago Press, 1944), pp. 103-04.

# 2

## Sovereignty and the State

To be sovereign is to have ultimate authority over the affairs of men. Sovereignty is at the heart of all social and political issues, and is a good starting point for our philosophical examination of these issues. As with most philosophical inquiries, however, we need first to examine a related family of concepts: society, the state, and government. The following brief discussion of these terms is not intended to lay out *the* definition of each, but to indicate the way in which they are used here.

### SOCIETY

The term *society* refers to a group of individuals living together. Two main features are necessary for a group to qualify as a society: The individuals in the group must be engaged in activity that is both cooperative and rule governed. Therefore, not all groups are societies.

For example, imagine a group of people living in close proximity. Each individual does as he chooses; there is no cooperation between these individuals; they do not work together; their actions are totally uncoordinated. A group of two-year-old children playing "together" illustrates this form of behavior. The children play in the same area, not really with each other, although they sometimes may be playing at the same game independently. Although such individuals are close to each other and their activities overlap, there is no cooperation among them, and hence the term *society* does not describe their group.

But the mere fact that a group of individuals work together in a cooperative fashion does not necessarily make them a society. After all, ants and bees cooperate and often with great precision. Yet there is an important difference between their "social" behavior and that of human beings. Perhaps this difference is best illustrated by the socialization of children. Early in development, children react primarily on a stimulus-response basis. Some of these responses are natural (e.g. crying when hungry) and some are learned (e.g. crying to attract attention), but because they only involve the stimulus-response mechanism, they are no different from the responses of lower-order animals.

As children grow older, they are taught to follow certain rules. The difference between the way animals and children follow rules is that, at some point, the child learns not merely to act in a certain way, but to act that way *because* a rule tells him he should. This is "rule governed behavior." Thus the individuals who constitute a society do not merely engage in cooperative activity; they engage in cooperative activity *that is rule governed.*

It follows that if a group of people engage in cooperative activity that is not rule governed, that group does not constitute a society. Moreover, although it may be difficult to imagine cooperation without rules, there is nothing logically contradictory about such a mode of interaction. A group of people can interact spontaneously—perhaps responding to each other through instinctive feelings of love—rather than on the basis of rules. If there were a community of angels, this mode would probably be theirs.

Even though it is logically possible for groups of people to behave in a loving way, without the use of rules, in actuality they do not. Without rules and rule-governed behavior, people contest rather than cooperate. This may be, as Hobbes believes (see ch. 4, § The Social Contract), because man's basic nature is contentious. Or it may be that, because conditions of scarcity have always prevailed, people are not satisfied, and so are in conflict with each other. But whatever the reason, it is an inescapable fact that all enduring cooperation involves rule-governed behavior.

This point highlights both the weakness and the strength of this use of the term *society.* Its weakness is that it precludes some logically possible arrangements from being called societies. Its strength, on the other hand, is that it focuses upon the features of cooperation and rule-governed behavior that seem essential in all existing societies. Since our concern is primarily with these features and these groups, it is desirable to use the term *society* in this way. If it becomes necessary to speak of groups that interact in a spontaneous rather than a rule-governed way—that is, to speak of all possible rather than all actual groups—some term other than *society* will have to be introduced.

## THE STATE

The term *state* is ambiguous. Sometimes it refers primarily to the political institutions or government of a group of people. In this sense, "the state of Maine" refers to the government and governors of the area designated as Maine. At other times the term refers primarily to the people, considered as a group, who live in Maine. It is in the latter sense that we use the word *state*.

Therefore, whatever else it may be, the state appears to be a society. But so too are families, fraternal organizations, churches, political parties, etc. What is it that distinguishes these forms of society from the state? First, most associations or societies are voluntary in the sense that one must join them to be a member, and can always resign if he so desires. Fraternities, clubs, churches, etc. all possess this characteristic. But one is a member of a state by virtue of being born there, and the only way to get out of being a member is to emigrate. Not only is leaving a state usually a great price to pay (often one must leave his possessions), but with immigration and emigration laws it is not always possible.

Second, the state tends to be the most general form of society. People join voluntary associations or smaller societies in the hope of achieving something in a particular area of life. The church is primarily religious; a labor union (although membership is not always voluntary) is primarily economic; a political party political; a sewing club recreational, and so on. But the state is a more general association than any of these. What unites people in a state is a common concern for survival and comfortable living, and a general agreement as to the way these goals should be pursued. In other words, certain concerns are important (e.g. religious, economic, political, or what have you), and certain basic rules need to be followed in pursuing these concerns. Sufficient agreement on these most general matters renders a group of people *a state*.

Thus we see that the state is a group of people engaged in cooperative rule-governed activity for the purpose of pursuing the most general aims of life. These same people, however, are also individuals. Thus arises the question: What is the relationship between the state (the group) and the individuals who make it up? Do not be put off because this question is abstract; much depends upon how one answers it.

### The State and the Individual:
### Atomistic and Organic Theories

The two main conceptions which provide answers to this question are the atomistic and organic theories of the state. In the atomistic theory, the state is simply the sum total of the individuals (or atoms) who make it up. To observe the behavior of the state, you simply observe the behavior of the individuals in it. Such views tend to place heavy emphasis on individualism because all there is to the state is the individuals who make it up.

In the organic theory, on the other hand, the state is like an organism in the respect that it is more than simply the sum total of its parts. The parts or cells of an organism come and go, but the organism endures. An organism unifies into a whole all the cells that have ever been, are, or will be part of it.

To see the differences between the atomistic and organic theories of the state, consider the following: Suppose it were possible to take a person apart cell by cell. Suppose further that somebody with meticulous care not only took Humpty apart cell by cell, but carefully labeled and stored each cell. Not knowing his fate, you ask "Where's Humpty?" and are shown the collection of cells. Most likely you respond, "But that can't be him!" If your point is simply that you do not recognize Humpty because his parts are not in the proper order—i.e. the collection of cells may be Humpty, although they need to be rearranged in order for you to recognize them as such—then you are viewing Humpty atomistically. If, on the other hand, your point is that there is more to Humpty than the cells that make him up, that there is also some kind of transcending element that gives unity to these parts, then you are viewing Humpty organically.

Analogously, according to the organic theory the state is more than the sum total of the individuals who make it up. The state unifies all generations—past, present, and future—into a whole which is greater than the sum of all its people. By being part of this whole, more than fleeting significance is attached to individual lives. It should not be surprising that such views, in contrast to the rugged individualism characteristic of atomistic theories, tend to emphasize the state rather than the individual.[1]

The atomistic view, on the other hand, reduces the concept of the state to the individuals who make it up, and the focus of concern changes from something seemingly vague and abstract (i.e. the state), to something much easier to observe and to study (i.e. the individual). In studying individuals one is studying part of the state, and the study of all individuals exhausts the study of the state.

Yet it may be that this advantage is purchased at the expense of obscuring the true nature of the state. Just as there seems to be more to Humpty than a collection of cells, so there seems to be more to the state than a collection of individuals. Thus, to conceive of the state simply as a group of individuals may ignore its true nature—that it unifies all individuals into a whole. But if one is going to speak of a transcending unity more than the sum total of the parts, then one must explain the nature of this unity. Thus the basic problem facing proponents of the organic theory is to give substance or content to the concept of an organic unity.

## GOVERNMENT

Regardless of whether one views the state atomistically or organically, there must be a way of establishing and enforcing the rules by which the members live. In other words, laws must be enacted and enforced. Government is the formal machinery for exercising this power or authority. When power is only exercised informally, there is no government. When it is exercised formally—when institutions, roles, channels, etc., are set up and used—there is a government.

Most families, for example, do not have governments. Although they have clearly established power relationships—in most cases the parents have the power and the children try to get around that power—these relationships are usually not formalized. There are no rules which set down who has the power to do what; there is no formalized judiciary to pass judgment on the behavior of the members, and no enforcement agency to catch the violators of the established rules. But most organizations—whether religious, fraternal, or political—do have governments, with constitutions or bylaws. They have formalized ways of establishing rules and dealing with violators of those rules.

The government of a social club provides the formal machinery for electing officers, setting and collecting dues, planning get-togethers, etc. The government of a state, supplies the machinery for increasing the chances of survival and comfortable living. It does so by providing the vehicle through which laws are enacted and enforced, and thus facilitates rule-governed behavior and cooperative activity.

What should be the relationship between government and the state? Some philosophers maintain that the state cannot exist without government because, given human nature, cooperation among men is impossible unless the strong arm of a government keeps everyone in line. Others maintain that, although the state is possible without government, the ability to cooperate sucessfully is greatly enhanced by the existence of government. Still others insist that not only is the state possible without government, it is most healthy without it. Each of these views is examined in some detail later on (ch. 4).

The important point here is that the terms *state* and *government* refer to decidedly different concepts. The former is primarily social, having its origins in the idea of society. The basic problem of the state is: Who does or should determine what the most general common interests and needs of the people are and how they should be pursued? On the other hand, the concept of government is primarily political. The basic problem of government is: What formal structure will most effectively allow for the determination and pursuit of the common interests and needs of the people by the appropriate authority?

## *SOVEREIGNTY*

These problems bring us to the central political issue of sovereignty, of political power. The basic question of sovereignty is: Who is or should be the appropriate power or authority? But there is an ambiguity here. If the focus is on who the power or authority *is,* then the question is raised at the descriptive level. If the focus is on who it *should be*, then the question is raised at the normative level.

In order to see how this ambiguity functions, we examine the concepts of power and authority. To have power over $X$ is to control him. To the extent that a teacher can tell his students what to do and they do it *because* he tells them to, he has power over them. To the extent that they simply ignore his words, or at least do not do what he says *because* he says it, he does not have power over them. In the descriptive approach to power, we look at existing institutions and explain the power relationships that prevail within them, and we determine which institutional arrangements are most conducive to the efficient exercise of power.

In the normative approach, on the other hand, we ask whether power can be justified. In its more general form, this question is: Does anyone have the right to exercise power or control over anyone else? In its more particular form, the question asks which particular powers may rightfully be exercised over whom by whom. I shall use the term *authority* to refer to this normative use of power. Therefore, to have authority over $X$ is to have the right to control him.

Power and authority can be related in four different ways:

1. A person may have both power and authority.
2. A person may have neither power nor authority.
3. A person may have power but not authority.
4. A person may have authority but not power.

In order to see how each of these possibilities works in practice, let us consider a platoon of soldiers.

If the platoon is well organized and well drilled, the commanding officer issues orders that the rest of the men carry out without question. Not only do the men follow the orders of their commander, but his right to command is legitimized by military law. Hence the commanding officer has both power and authority (the right to exercise power) over his men. Moreover, should some other member of the platoon give an order without the approval of the commanding officer, the other men in the unit would not follow it; nor, according to military law, should they. Hence other members of the platoon have neither power nor authority over their fellow soldiers.

But suppose that the platoon is not so well trained. Suppose that when they enter into battle things do not go well for them. They are getting cut to ribbons by the enemy, but the commanding officer tells them to push on. Suddenly one of the men in the platoon decides that he has had enough. He starts to retreat, calling for the others to follow him. In spite of the orders of the commanding officer to the contrary, the rest of the men follow his lead. For a short time they follow their new leader in the same way they had been taught to follow their commanding officer. This new leader has gained power but not authority over his fellow soldiers. By the same token, the commanding officer has lost power. Assuming he has not done anything which according to military law results in his losing the right to command his men, he still has the right to exercise control over them. Hence even though he has lost power, he still has authority.

Notice that this example bases authority or the right to control on military law. But one need not do this. It is always possible to question the legitimacy of military law itself. One can always say that although according to military law $X$ has the right to control, military law is not the appropriate norm, and hence $X$ does not have authority. Crucial here is that the role of philosophy is to question rather than simply to accept normative standards. Notice that, once one accepts *military law* as the basis of authority, whether or not a given act is legitimate becomes a descriptive question, and is answered by determining whether or not the act is in accordance with this law. But the salient philosophical issue is the normative question, Should military law be accepted as the standard of legitimacy? Hence our concern with the concept of authority is not with the question of who, according to accepted standards, has authority over what, but rather with what the standards for authority should be—i.e., Who should have authority over what?

As we have seen, the term *sovereignty* functions ambiguously. If you study institutions descriptively in the *de facto* sense, you normally use sovereign to refer to where the ultimate power actually lies in those institutions. If, on the other hand, you study institutions normatively in the *de jure* sense, your concern is to determine where the *right to power* or *authority* lies, and you normally use the term to refer to the ultimate authority. Because the concern of this book is normative, the term *sovereignty* is used primarily in the *de jure* or normative sense.

To see this distinction more clearly, consider the parent-child relationship. In this relationship the parent (at least initially) is sovereign. Even the most permissive parents retain ultimate power. When push comes to shove, at least in the early years, the parents have the final say. As children develop, their parents usually give them a greater and greater say over particular decisions that affect them. Yet this larger voice is merely an exercise—training them to be on their own. Should a child make a bad decision, the parent has the power to step in and take over, for it is the parent who is sovereign. At some point, most young people start to rebel against the power of their parents and seek to assert control over their own lives. Sometimes this battle takes years, sometimes less. But eventually young people overcome the sovereignty of their parents and control their own lives.

This analysis of the parent-child relationship has been entirely descriptive in nature. It merely attempts to indicate where ultimate power lies at various stages in the relationship. Every time the term *sovereign* appears, *de facto* sovereignty is referred to. But this same relationship can be analyzed very differently. It could have been asserted that when children are young their parents have the right to exercise control over their lives, but that there comes a point at which this right passes from the parent to the child (it may or may not coincide with the passing of actual control). The appearance of the term *sovereign* in this analysis, because authority rather than power is at issue, refers to normative or *de jure* sovereignty.

Thus the basic question of sovereignty is: Who *should* have ultimate authority over the affairs of men? The myriad of answers that have been given to this question fall into three main species—the theories of dictatorial, popular, and individual sovereignty. We now examine each of these theories in turn.

### Dictatorial Sovereignty

The basic idea of dictatorial sovereignty is that one person, or a limited group of persons, has ultimate authority, and thus the right to dictate what the people should do. More interesting, however, are the two ways in which thinkers attempt to justify the dictator's authority: he gets it either from God or by virtue of possessing very special abilities.

One of the earliest forms is the theocratic state. There the dictator is chosen by God to see that his will be done, and this will is transmitted to the ruler either directly or through an intermediary (i.e. a priest). The most important species of this theory is the doctrine of "the divine right of kings."

### Rule by Divine Right

Although historically the divine right of kings is usually passed from parent to child, there is no logical connection between the view that the king is God's agent on earth and the idea that his child should succeed him. There is no reason why upon the death of his earthly agent God could not select a new one, rather than simply accepting the old agent's offspring as his successor. Of course this would greatly complicate the practical side of things; whenever a king died there would undoubtedly be a struggle to see who could claim the role of God's new agent. But the basic idea behind the doctrine of the divine right of kings is that the king rules because he is chosen by God, not simply because he is a member of a certain family.

Two points must be made about this species of the theory of dictatorial sovereignty. The first is that, as a justification of the right to rule, it can only have significance for those with a theological world-view. To those who reject the idea of God or, more correctly, of a personal God who guides the affairs of men, such a justification carries no weight at all. Of course if you believe in a personal God you do not have to accept the doctrine of the divine right of kings. There is nothing at all contradictory about believing in God and rejecting the idea of divine right—you may simply feel that God has created men to be ruled by themselves rather than by Him, or you may believe that God rules over the world directly rather than by means of an intermediary (i.e. the king). But any argument that begins with the concept of God can have no persuasive power at all for those who reject that concept.

Second, although God is omnipotent and hence has the power to rule over us, He does not necessarily have the right to. Of course many thinkers claim that God is all-good as well as all-powerful and argue that his goodness justifies his authority. But one must still come to grips with the kind of objection raised by Sartre in his essay, "Existentialism as a Humanism."[2] In this essay Sartre argues that even if God exists, He has no right to interfere with our lives; such interference undermines individual freedom. Of course one can attempt to refute Sartre's argument in a variety of ways—for example, show that the nature of freedom is such that God's authority is not incompatible with human freedom. But this is beside the point. The relationship between God's existence and his authority is problematic, and hence the move from his existence to his authority must be explained and justified.

### Rule by Truth of Philosopher King

The next justification given for the theory of dictatorial sovereignty does not invoke the notion of God at all. The idea here is that certain individuals are able to perceive what is best for the people. If the people were to make their own decisions, they would make very bad ones. Hence ultimate authority should be vested in the hands of those who know what is best, for in this way the people will be better off than they otherwise could be.

Probably the most famous, and certainly the most eloquent, proponent of this argument is Plato. In *The Republic* he presents his view of the ideal state, ruled by the absolute hand of the wisest man in the land, the philosopher king. Plato supports this view of the state with an elaborate **epistemological** theory, about the nature and possibility of having knowledge. The basic idea of this theory is that the fundamental truths of life are eternal and unchanging (Plato calls these truths "forms"). Of course men live best when they live according to these truths. But the average man (indeed, even the above average man) is incapable of perceiving these forms. Left to themselves, men live very differently from the way they should. Thus it is necessary to find a way to have men live according to the eternal truths of life.

It will not do simply to have someone tell them what these eternal truths are. For the average man could not see their truth even then. Hence needed is someone with both the capability of perceiving the forms and the power to get men to live by them. This function belongs to the philosopher king. He is capable of perceiving the forms; he has developed this capacity by a long, arduous period of training and competition with others. He also has the right to rule over the people. This authority is justified because only in this way can the people live in accordance with the forms, and only when they are so living can they do as they should.

The basic problem with this attempt to justify dictatorial sovereignty is epistemological; Plato's version of the theory makes this fact crystal clear. In theory, truth (or the forms) is sovereign, and the philosopher king is the only one who can discover the truth. Thus, even if we set aside the question of whether or not there are any eternal and unchanging truths, the philosopher king is still the only one capable of perceiving them, and hence the people must accept whatever he says as true. If there are such truths and if he rules in accordance with them, there may be no problem. But what guarantees do the people have that the king perceives and rules in accordance with them? They have no way of knowing whether or not he is deceiving them. In effect whatever the ruler deems right is right (i.e. the ruler is sovereign), even though the system is developed within a theory where truth is sovereign.

A second important objection to this theory is similar to Sartre's argument against the sovereignty of God. Some thinkers claim that even if Plato is right, even if there are eternal truths and an individual who can perceive them, there is no justification for that individual to rule over everyone else. Individual freedom or autonomy is more important than living by the truth. In other words, even if an individual is going to make the wrong decision, the choice should be left up to him. In this view, for one individual to impose his will on others is tyranny or oppression, and the fact that he is the wisest person in the land and is doing it in the name of truth does not make it any less so.

### Popular Sovereignty

In this view ultimate authority rests in the hands of the people. Each individual does not have ultimate authority over his own affairs (individual sovereignty), but the people as a group have ultimate authority over everyone's affairs. In other words, all individual rights are granted by the people, and can be repealed by the people at any time. Ultimate authority rests with the people, and a way must be found to translate their will into the law of the land.

The typical way of doing this is through the ballot box. The easiest way to interpret the vote is to equate the idea of the will of the people with a fixed percentage of votes. Most often this figure is set at a simple majority, although there is no reason why a smaller figure (e.g. a plurality) or a larger figure (e.g. a two-thirds majority) cannot be used. There are also more complicated alternatives such as plural voting (giving some individuals more than one vote), the electoral college system used in U.S. presidential elections, and so on. The lower we set the percentage that represents the will of the people, the harder it is to maintain that the vote represents that will. At some point popular sovereignty leaves off and dictatorial sovereignty (rule by a limited group) begins.

### The Right to Revolution

The people may either vote on particular issues directly through national referendums or they may vote for officials who make these decisions. In the latter case, steps must be taken to protect the sovereignty of the people (i.e. prevent the elected officials from ruling as they choose, rather than as the people want them to). The most-often-used safeguard is to require all elected officials to stand for reelection periodically. Another is to make the elected officials subject to recall should the people become unhappy with them. The ultimate safeguard is the right to revolution. Under popular sovereignty whenever it is possible for officials (elected or otherwise) to usurp the power of the people, and thereby violate the people's authority, the people have the right to throw the usurpers out. This right is part of what it means for the people to be sovereign (i.e. that they have the *right* to have control over their affairs).

The right to revolution has been given its clearest formulation by John Locke.

Whensoever, therefore, the legislative shall transgress this fundamental rule of society, and either by ambition, fear, folly, or corruption, endeavor to grasp themselves, or put into the hands of any other, an absolute power over the lives, liberties, and estates of the people, by this breach of trust they forfeit the power the people had put into their hands for quite contrary ends, and it devolves to the people, who have the right to resume their original liberty and, by the establishment of a new legislative, such as they shall think fit, provide for their own safety and security, which is the end for which they are in society. What I have said here concerning the legislative in general holds true also concerning the supreme executor, . . .[3]

We need to look closely at this right to revolution. First of all, it is a "right." It does *not* make the descriptive claim that if a government becomes too oppressive the people *will* in fact seek to throw off the yoke through a revolution. Rather, the right to revolution makes the normative claim that there are certain conditions under which the people are *justified* in overthrowing their government.

Secondly, as Locke made quite clear,[4] the people should use this right judiciously. If they were to revolt at every little difference of opinion with their leaders, the result would be chaos. But when their leaders consistently ignore their desires and interests, then the people should rise up and throw the scoundrels out. Without this right, the people would not be truly sovereign.

Finally, it is "the people" rather than individuals or groups of individuals who have the right to revolution. When their power is usurped, the people have the right to take it back. Thus the right to revolution, at least as far as the theory of popular sovereignty is concerned, is simply the right of the people to assert their sovereignty in the event that their power is somehow taken from them. It has nothing to do with the right of oppressed minorities to throw off the yoke of their oppressors.

This point is important. Popular sovereignty is the view that the people have ultimate authority. Since there is seldom unanimous agreement among people, there will invariably be some individuals who are opposed to what the people decide, and who will feel that the will of the people is being imposed upon them. In particular cases such an imposition may or may not be tyrannical. But just as dictatorial sovereignty opens the door to tyranny of the few (or minority), so popular sovereignty opens the door to tyranny of the people (or majority). And the right to revolution, at least as understood by Locke and other proponents of popular sovereignty, offers no protection against this form of tyranny.

Proponents of popular sovereignty respond to this problem in a variety of ways. Some insist that it is simply a necessary evil of social life. Decisions must be made—and if unanimity were required nothing would ever be decided. Hence the fairest thing to do is abide by something like majority rule, even if the result is the imposition of the will of the majority upon the minority. Others insist that it is necessary to provide some protection to minority rights. However, to the extent that they extend rights to minorities that cannot be taken away by the majority, they are comprising the theory of popular sovereignty.

To see this point, imagine a system in which minority rights are granted by a constitution which can be amended by the people. In this case the people retain their sovereignty but minorities are not really protected because the people (i.e. the majority) can take their rights away whenever they want to do so. If, on the other hand, minority rights are granted by a vehicle such as a constitution which cannot be amended, then minorities are protected but the sovereignty of the people is compromised. For although the people may still be sovereign within the limits defined by the constitution, the constitution establishes an area in which the majority is not sovereign.

But not all thinkers respond to the threat of the tyranny of the majority by attempting to amend or defend the theory of popular sovereignty. Some feel that it is popular sovereignty itself that is the problem, and hence it is popular sovereignty that must go. It is their view that as long as anyone has the right to impose his will on someone else, something is amiss. What these thinkers advocate is a system in which "the individual" rather than "the people" is sovereign.

### Individual Sovereignty

Whereas both dictatorial and popular sovereignty give ultimate authority to an individual or a group, individual sovereignty gives each individual ultimate authority over himself. You have probably come across this theory under the more popular name of anarchism.

The theory of individual sovereignty or anarchism is not necessarily incompatible with the state as we have defined it. The theory requires that the ideas of cooperative activity and rule-governed behavior be spelled out in such a way that they do not interfere with the voluntary activities of the members of the state. No one can be forced to cooperate, to follow rules he does not accept. An anarchistic state must be founded on cooperative activities that everyone wants to take part in, and on social rules that every individual sets down for himself.

Although some anarchists accept the idea of the state as we have defined it, all anarchists reject the idea of government. As they see it, the basic function of the formal structure of government is to facilitate imposing the will of some people on everyone else. According to the anarchist, the forces of repression (the police, the military, the courts, etc.) are the essence of government. Of course these have no place in a society based entirely upon the idea of voluntary action. Moreover, even if it were possible to have a government that is in no way repressive, government is still undesirable. The mere existence of a structure through which it is possible to exercise power over individuals makes it highly likely that at some point this power will be exercised. In other words, not only is government not necessary; its mere existence provides too much of a temptation to violate individual sovereignty.

The basic problem in the theory of individual sovereignty is almost too obvious to mention. There is just too much disagreement and conflict among people. As we shall see (ch. 4), some thinkers maintain that cooperation is impossible without the existence of a strong ruler who has the power to make people cooperate. Others maintain that although some cooperation is possible when individuals are sovereign, this cooperation cannot go very far without the institution of majority rule. The idea of cooperative rule-governed activity involves not merely the acceptance of a set of rules, but the sticking by those rules even when you don't feel like it or when it is not particularly to your advantage to do so. But who would do this if there were no enforcement agency to make him?

This same point is often made in another way. We have already seen that dictatorial sovereignty raises the problem of tyranny of the minority whereas popular sovereignty raises the problem of tyranny of the majority. It is often claimed that individual sovereignty raises the problem of tyranny of the strong. In other words, where there is no authorized enforcement agency, the strong will impose their will upon the weak. Not that they are justified in doing so. Indeed, given that everyone has authority over himself, such domination is clearly unjustified. But given the way people are, this kind of thing is bound to happen.

In other words, the theory of individual sovereignty or anarchism makes the issue of tyranny practical. On the theoretical level there can be no tyranny because all imposition of will by one person upon another is illegitimate. On the practical level, however, there is a problem—one must determine whether or not there will in fact be impositions of will when there is no authority to stop them. In dictatorial and popular sovereignty, however, the situation is just the opposite. The issue of tyranny is not practical, since in these views whatever the sovereign does is legitimate rather than oppressive (of course this does not mean that there cannot be usurpation of power). But the issue of tyranny does arise on the theoretical level—i.e. one can claim that these theories of sovereignty, because they allow for the imposition of the will of some upon others, are themselves tyrannical.

### Mixed Theories of Sovereignty

Logically, dictatorial, popular, and individual sovereignty are distinct theories, but they can be mixed together. In actual fact, you most often find such mixtures. Consider popular sovereignty, for example. Some of the thinkers who claim that the people are sovereign also maintain that there are some areas of private life (morality, finances, etc.) where the people have no right to interfere; they combine individual with popular sovereignty. Others maintain that there are some agencies (the military, courts, etc.) that must be independent of the people in order to operate effectively;[5] they combine dictatorial with popular sovereignty. We are not at the moment concerned with which view is correct. The important point is that dictatorial, popular, and individual sovereignty seldom appear in their pure forms.

In whatever form sovereignty takes, the individual must lose some of his freedom—to the dictator, the people, or the strong. It is time now to examine the concept of freedom.

## NOTES

1. The dichotomy between atomistic and organic theories of the state has its direct analogue in individualistic and holistic theories of society. This of course is just what you would expect (given that the state is a society).

2. See Jean-Paul Sartre, *Existentialism and Human Emotions,* trans. Bernard Frechtman and Hazel E. Barnes (New York: Citadel Press, 1957), pp. 9-52.

3. John Locke, *The Second Treatise of Government* (Indianapolis: Bobbs-Merrill, 1952), p. 124.

4. Ibid., p. 126.

5. Some recent U.S. presidents have been accused of thinking that this is true of their office as well.

# 3

## *Freedom*

In any kind of state the individual suffers some loss of freedom. This realization brings us to a key question in social and political thought; How and to what extent is it possible for an individual to live in society (i.e. engage in rule-governed cooperative activity) and yet be free? In addition to this sociopolitical problem of freedom, there is also the **metaphysical** problem.

Metaphysics is the study of the basic nature of reality. As such it is concerned with the most fundamental questions imaginable: Is there a God? Are human beings composed of both mind and matter or just one of them? Does every event have a cause? Is there any such thing as free will or free choice? The latter is the focus of the metaphysician's concern with the concept of freedom.

Although it may not appear so at first glance, the metaphysical and the sociopolitical approaches to freedom are closely related. The sociopolitical problem presupposes that freedom is possible. If it is not, then of course an individual cannot live in society and be free. If, moreover, the freedom that concerns social and political philosophers is the same as the metaphysician's notion of free choice,[1] then the question Is social freedom possible? presupposes an answer to the question Do human beings have free choice?

In other words, if there is no such thing as free choice, then everything an individual does is the result of factors and conditions over which he has no control. The decision to go swimming is no more within one's control than is being pushed into a swimming pool. But if this is so, then it is hard to see a significant difference between being forced to do something (by another individual or the state) and being left alone to do it. In other words, there does not seem to be any content to the notion of sociopolitical freedom.

Perhaps this point is made more clearly by use of another example. Consider the difference between an individual who violates the law and one who violates the law while under the spell of someone else (perhaps acting under the influence of a posthypnotic suggestion). Normally we would want to punish the first individual and excuse the second. Moreover, if there is such a thing as free choice this decision is easy to justify—we simply point out that the one individual acted freely while the other did not. But if there is no such thing as free choice, we cannot say this. Moreover, when pressed, it is hard to think of any way at all to distinguish between the two acts. The first individual acted under the "spell" of his environment, while the second acted under the "spell" of another individual. In order to justify punishing the first, but not the second, we must argue that there is a difference between acting under the influence of the forces of nature and under the influence of people, which justifies punishing those who are under the influence of the former and excusing those who are under the influence of the latter. If there is no such difference, then there is no way to justify the desired duality of treatment.

Without introducing the notion of free choice, I see no way to draw the distinction between acting under the influence of nature and of people. But it would take us too far afield for me to go into the arguments. It is sufficient to realize that, if I am correct, metaphysical freedom is more fundamental than sociopolitical. Hence, any answer to the sociopolitical question presupposes an answer to the metaphysical question. Because there is at least some reason for thinking I am correct, it is desirable to begin our discussion with the meta-physical problem of freedom. Furthermore, before one can adequately answer either question, one must have some idea of what "freedom" means. Although this definition is invariably discussed in metaphysics (partly because the context readily lends itself to such an analysis), very often those involved with the sociopolitical question simply presuppose such an account without ever devel-oping it. This, of course, can lead to much confusion. By beginning with the metaphysical problem we both lay bare the presuppositions of and provide the conceptual basis necessary for giving an adequate answer to the question: *How and to what extent is it possible for an individual to live in society and yet be free?*

## THE METAPHYSICAL PROBLEM

Metaphysics asks the question of freedom, Is there any such thing as free will or free choice? Many philosophers say no, and they base their reasoning on the dilemma that grows out of the relationship between free choice and determinism or indeterminism (or both).

### Determinism

The determinist's view is that *nothing* can possibly happen without a cause—that is, everything that happens is brought about by something which preceded it, and given what happened before it, that thing had to happen. Think back to when you were a child, at some point while you were playing, you undoubtedly set up a long row of blocks, each on its edge. Then you tipped the first one over and watched with glee as the inevitable chain reaction occurred. Each block fell into the one next to it until all that was left was a jumbled mess of blocks on the floor.

Note two important things about such a chain reaction. First, the place where each individual block ends up is completely determined by the interaction between two different kinds of factors—the situation in which the block is placed (i.e. its location vis-a-vis the other blocks, the nature of the terrain, etc.) and the force that is exerted on it (by the other blocks, the force of gravity, etc.). The question of uncaused events does not arise. Each block simply responds mechanically, in accordance with the physical laws of the universe, to the forces exerted upon it. Second, if we were to know all the causal laws and factors relevant to blocks and their behavior (e.g. the weight and shape of each block, the speed at which the first block begins to fall, the velocity and direction of the wind, and so on), we would be able to predict exactly where each block would be at every moment. In other words, the behavior of the blocks is *in principle* predictable—we can accurately predict their behavior if we have the requisite information.

The thesis of determinism is that the entire universe is the block situation writ large. It does not matter how the universe was created, it functions the way that the blocks do. For most people, this claim is perfectly reasonable for the world of nature; that is, if we leave human beings out of the picture, the universe works on the model of our blocks. But the determinist goes much further; he insists that human activity is every bit as determined as the world of nature. He points out that the causal laws that govern human activity are far more complex and obscure than those that govern nonhuman activity; it is only because of our ignorance of these laws that we think that human acts are uncaused. With the establishment of psychology as a science and with the growth this science is experiencing, people are coming to see that human actions are as much governed by causal laws as are the events of nature. They will soon realize that, just as there are no uncaused events in the world of nature, so there are no uncaused choices in the world of human activity.

The significance of this point must not be underestimated. If the determinist is correct, then there is no significant difference between committing suicide and being killed in a natural disaster. True, in one case you are dying at your own hands while in the other you are dying at the hands of the forces of nature. But you have no more control over your own actions than you do over the forces of nature. Both your own actions and those of nature are the result of causal factors over which you have no control. Your suicide is just one more event in the inexorable chain reaction which is the universe. In short, all your choices are in effect made for you by causal forces over which you have no control. Hence, there is no such thing as a free choice.

### Indeterminism

Faced with this line of argument some philosophers have turned to indeterminism in an attempt to preserve the notion of free choice. Indeterminism is the view that there are some (at least one) events that do not have a cause. Most indeterminists accept the determinist's account of the world of nature. But they insist that human beings make free choices.

They say that human acts of will (i.e. deliberative choices) are uncaused, and hence they are free. We can see immediately that equating "uncaused" with "free" is not without its problems. Imagine yourself sitting in an ice cream parlor trying to decide what to order; after much deliberation you narrow the choice down to either a hot fudge sundae or a banana split. And you finally decide on the sundae. According to the determinist, for every step in your deliberative process there were causal factors which necessitated your choosing the sundae.

The indeterminist would claim, however, that at least one of the steps in this process—we will consider just the final choice— is uncaused. Up to the time you choose between the hot fudge sundae and the banana split, you can choose either of the two delicacies. Moreover, there is no cause of your choice of the sundae. But this suggests that your choice is simply a chance occurrence which happens *to you* rather than something that you bring about. And surely this is not what people have in mind when they speak of free choice or free will! Such chance occurrences are as much outside our control as acts brought about by causal factors. Thus it seems that indeterminism is as incompatible with free choice as determinism—even though they are incompatible for quite different reasons.

### Reconciling the Dilemma of Determinism

In a dilemma a given conclusion must be true because it follows from both a thesis *and* the denial of that thesis (one of which must be true). Hence the conclusion is true regardless of whether you accept the thesis or not. In short, you're damned if you do and you're damned if you don't. The dilemma of choice. If indeterminism is true, then there is no such thing as free choice. Either determinism or indeterminism is true. Therefore there is no such thing as free choice.

There are two ways to attack a dilemma: either show that the two horns of the dilemma are not the only alternatives or that one of the horns must be rejected. In our particular case, the former would mean arguing that determinism and indeterminism are not the only possibilities; the latter would involve arguing that free choice is compatible with either determinism *or* indeterminism. Given that indeterminism is defined as the denial of determinism, the first line of argument would be singularly unsuccessful. So it is that philosophers who desire to maintain the existence of free choice have taken the second alternative and have attempted to reconcile free choice with either determinism or indeterminism.

### Compatibilism

Theories that attempt to reconcile free choice with determinism go under a variety of names. The two most popular are compatibilism and soft determinism.

The basic idea in all such views is that people believe there is a conflict between free choice and determinism because they are confused about what a free choice is. They mistakenly believe that in order for a choice to be free it must be uncaused; of course if this belief is so, then free choice and determinism (the view that every event has a cause) must be incompatible. But if we look at the way the terms *free* and *freedom* are used in everyday discourse, we see that this meaning is not conveyed by the terms.

Normally, when we speak of being free we have in mind, not that an act is uncaused (contracausal freedom), but rather that we have been able to do what we choose. In other words, no external constraints prevent our translating choices into actions. Thus a person in a locked room is not free to leave, whereas a person in an unlocked room is free to leave. A person pinned under the wreckage of a car is unfree whereas a person simply lying under a car is free. A person who is killed does not die freely whereas a person who takes his own life does die freely. And so on. And this freedom is independent of whether the act has been "determined" or "undetermined." The compatibilist concludes, therefore, that the question of whether an act is free is different from the question of whether that act is caused.

The compatibilist contends then that, when we look carefully at the word *free*, we see that freedom and determinism are not incompatible. Although it is true that determinism is incompatible with contracausal freedom, it is not the contracausal sense of freedom that applies to free choices. All we normally mean when we use the term *free* in this context is that there are no external constraints which prevent our translating our choices into actions, and the presence or absence of such constraints has nothing at all to do with whether or not the choice is caused.

Although this attempt to reconcile freedom and determinism is both interesting and suggestive, it is not without its problems. The basic problem is that although there may be a difference between a choice being free and uncaused, the equating of freedom with the absence of external constraints does not seem to be an adequate way of drawing this distinction. To see this, consider the case of a compulsive handwasher. He washes his hands because they feel dirty to him, but they feel dirty to him hundreds of times a day. Now there seems to be a difference between the actions of a compulsive handwasher and the actions of a normal handwasher; and this difference is at least partially captured by saying that the compulsive does not wash his hands freely whereas the noncompulsive does.

The problem is, however, that if free is defined as the absence of *external* constraints, then we cannot say this. The constraints operative on the compulsive are internal rather than external. Hence if we want to continue to distinguish between constraints and causes as the compatibilist does, we must find a way to distinguish all constraints (both internal and external) from causes.

Unfortunately, however, no really satisfactory way of distinguishing the kinds of constraints operative on the compulsive from the everyday forces that are operative on everyone has been found. Therefore, compatibilism does not provide a completely adequate way of reconciling freedom and determinism.

### Libertarianism

The second way that philosophers have attempted to resolve the dilemma of determinism is by trying to show that free choice is not really incompatible with indeterminism. This position is often called libertarianism. As we saw in the fudge sundae example, indeterminism is said to be incompatible with free choice on the grounds that an uncaused event must be a random or chance occurrence, and a random or chance occurrence is no more a free choice than is a completely determined event. The libertarian, then, tries to show how an act or a choice can be both uncaused (he accepts the idea that "free" means uncaused) and yet free.

As a result the libertarian argues that being caused and being random are not the only two alternatives. There is a middle ground, a ground on which there are acts or choices which are both uncaused and chosen—that is, the deliberative choices of the agent. These choices are what we call free. If is difficult, however, to see how an act can be both uncaused and chosen by someone. It would seem that either I cause a choice, in which case it is my choice, or else I do not cause the choice, in which case it is more like something that happens to me, and hence could not be my choice. At any rate, we have noted all that is essential for our purposes—viz. that the task that faces the libertarian is to try to show how an act can be both uncaused and someone's act.

This brief discussion of the dilemma of determinism in no way solves the metaphysical problem of freedom. It merely attempts to clarify the problem and outline its dialectic. We have seen that this approach to freedom is not merely abstract, it is fundamental. If one accepts the dilemma of determinism, thereby rejecting the very possibility of freedom, then there is a real question as to whether or not it makes sense to proceed to the sociopolitical dimensions of the problem. If, on the other hand, one rejects the dilemma on the basis that free choice is compatible with either determinism or indeterminism, then the question of social freedom is one that must be faced directly. Moreover, the analysis of the concept of freedom just presented is invaluable for understanding the sociopolitical aspect of the problem of freedom to which we now turn.

## THE SOCIOPOLITICAL PROBLEM

The dialectic which surrounds this problem has produced two different approaches. Some philosophers have been mainly concerned with what has come

to be called negative freedom, whereas others have been concerned with what
has come to be called positive freedom. Although there is some overlap between
the two concepts, there are also some vital differences—so vital, in fact, that
what is freedom under one concept is slavery under the other, and vice versa.
Hence it is imperative, if we are going to understand the discussions of freedom
by social and political philosophers, for us to grasp this distinction.[2]

### Negative Freedom

Probably the clearest, and certainly one of the most influential proponents of
the concept of negative freedom is John Stuart Mill. Writing in England in the
1860s, Mill was troubled about the growth of government and its involvement in
the everyday affairs of the people. He believed that the right of the government
(or individual citizens for that matter) to interfere in the lives of people must be
severely limited. In his famous nonintervention principle Mill states:

... the sole end for which mankind are warranted, individually or collectively,
in interfering with the liberty of action of any of their number is self-protection.
That the only purpose for which power can be rightfully exercised over any
member of a civilized community, against his will, is to prevent harm to others.
His own good, either physical or moral, is not a sufficient warrant.[3]

In other words, individuals or the group have the right to interfere with your
freedom of action (i.e. impose external constraints upon you) only when your
action will result in harm to others. If you want to do something that will not
harm anyone else (even though it may harm yourself), no one has the right to
interfere with you.

The greatest single problem in applying Mill's principle is determining what
constitutes "harm to others." It is plain that killing, assault, etc. involve such
harm and helping others, being courteous, etc. do not. But there are many other
cases that are not so clear. Suppose a woman commits suicide. Are her husband
and children harmed by her act? Suppose a man exposes himself in public. Are
the people affected by the sight harmed by his act? But these problems need not
detain us here since we discuss them in detail in chapter 6.

Mill views freedom as the absence of external constraints (as does the
compatibilist), and argues that the only reason for limiting a person's freedom is
to stop others from being harmed. One can disagree with Mill on either of these
grounds. If you deny that freedom is the absence of external constraints, then
you reject the concept of negative freedom. If you disagree on the second
ground—that the only reason for limiting freedom is to protect others from
harm—then you accept the concept of negative freedom. But you differ from
Mill about the conditions under which it is legitimate to limit that freedom.

With the idea of negative freedom now before us, some refinements are necessary. First, the idea of complete or absolute freedom must be rejected. Normally we live in situations where people are more or less free (more or less limited by external constraints). On one level this is perfectly obvious. The physical world imposes all sorts of limitations on us—we cannot breathe under water without the aid of some kind of apparatus, nor fly unassisted; we cannot change lead into gold, nor restore to life those who have died; a cripple cannot walk, nor can someone with a failing heart run up a flight of stairs. It is impossible for anyone to be completely free of constraints of this kind. Hence it is impossible for anyone to be absolutely free.

You may object at this point that it is not fair to call these kinds of limitations constraints on our freedom because they are part of the natural world, or part of the human condition. Only man-made constraints can rightfully be called limitations upon our freedom. Only when we are limited in what we can do by other people or institutions constructed by people (e.g. a government) can we properly speak of our freedom being limited.

### The Paradox of Freedom

Actually, nothing much turns on whether or not we restrict the term *freedom* to the limitations imposed by other people. Even if we do use freedom in this restricted way one individual within society, at most, can be absolutely free, and only by enslaving everyone else. All freedom is purchased at the expense of freedom. My freedom to live is a result of limiting the freedom of others to kill. My freedom to drink clean water depends upon preventing others from polluting the drinking water. My freedom of movement is a result of limiting the freedom of others to interfere with my movement, and so on. Perhaps the best way to decide which freedoms should be preserved and which given up is the "harm to others" test set down by Mill. Or perhaps this test is either inadequate or unacceptable—inadequate because there are some limitations that should be imposed even when there is no harm to others, unacceptable because there is some other criterion that should be used in deciding which limitations upon freedom are in order.

These examples, and the reasoning behind them, reveal the "paradox of freedom"—every freedom is purchased at the expense of some other freedom or freedoms. It follows that discussions of freedom for the most part are concerned with which or whose freedoms should be sacrificed and which or whose freedoms should be preserved, even though the discussions are often presented as disputes between the forces of freedom and of slavery. No wonder disputes involving freedom are so difficult to resolve!

*Freedom as a Function of the Options Available*

Because negative freedom involves the absence of external constraints, some
thinkers conclude that all freedom is *freedom from the interference of others.*
But others claim that there is also *the freedom to do things,* and that without
this latter a person is not really free. In this view, not only is freedom a function
of the elimination of external constraints, it is also a function of the number of
genuine options available.

Consider, the difference between a rich and a poor man. The rich man has
much freedom when it comes to choosing a vacation spot; the poor man,
because of his limited resources, has practically none. The rich can live in any
area of town he chooses but the poor is limited by what he can afford. The rich
has his choice of the foodstuffs available in the stores; the poor man is limited
by his food budget. And so on. Formally, of course everyone is entitled to
vacation wherever they choose, live where they want, purchase the food they
like, etc. But for the poor, these freedoms have a hollow ring—they exist in form
only. On the substantive or effective level, the freedom of the poor is considerably less than that of the rich simply because there are far fewer genuine options
open to the poor.

This point gives us a perspective from which to view many disputes involving
freedom. For example, some people believe that wealth should be distributed
through the free operation of the market place; others feel that a freely operating
marketplace does not distribute wealth equitably enough. In this dispute each
side usually claims to be the champion of freedom and charges their opponents
with advocating slavery. The supporters of a free marketplace speak of the
slavery of conscriptive taxation and government intervention in economic
affairs. Advocates of redistribution speak of the privilege of the rich and the
slavery of the masses. But now we can see that the issue is not one of slavery vs.
freedom. Rather it is, Should the formal freedom to invest and accumulate
wealth be limited in order to increase the genuine options available to the mass
of people? Those who advocate redistribution say Yes. Those who advocate the
free marketplace say, This freedom must be maintained even if it can only be
used by some people and even if it results in less effective freedom (fewer
genuine options) for the mass of people.

Thus the problem of negative freedom is not simply whether or not people
should be subjected to external constraints. Given the paradox of freedom, all
people have external constraints imposed on them. Rather the question of
negative freedom is, Which set of constraints should be imposed as a means of
preserving which set of freedoms?

Before we turn to the concept of positive freedom please note that the terms
*positive* and *negative* freedom sometimes are used to refer respectively to what I
have just labeled *effective* and *formal* freedom. It seems to me, however, that
"formal" and "effective" are far more descriptive of this distinction and that

"positive" and "negative" are most descriptive of the distinction between external and internal constraints; hence it is preferable to use these terms in the way I have been using them.


### Positive Freedom

All the problems considered so far arise from viewing freedom as the absence of external constraint. One might well wonder if this condition is all there is to freedom. It does seem that being unfettered and having sufficient opportunities is at least part of what is meant by freedom; a person locked in a room certainly seems to be unfree. But is being unfettered all that is required for freedom? Is it possible for someone to be both unfettered (in the sense we have been considering) and unfree? The proponents of positive freedom believe that the answer to this question is Yes. Although their reasoning may not be obvious at first glance, a couple of examples should help make clear why they take this view.

Imagine a soldier who has just returned home from a prisoner-of-war camp. At the time of his capture he was 100 percent love-it-or-leave-it American. His country could do no wrong, and he wanted every other nation in the world to recognize this fact. He returns a changed man; he becomes increasingly concerned about American imperialism and our militaristic posture throughout the world. At home, he is worried about the military-industrial complex and the specter of American fascism. As a result he begins questioning (and even protesting against) some of the decisions made by our country's leaders.

Of course we all "know" what the trouble is—this soldier was brainwashed while a prisoner-of-war. The implications for the concept of freedom are very significant. There are no apparent external constraints operative on him, and yet in a very real sense the acts he performs upon his return home are not really free. After all, this is not the way he normally behaves. Some *internal* constraints operating on him render his actions unfree. Only when he is rid of the terrible forces that control him can we call him free.

In the case of brainwashing we can always point to an external constraint, the brainwashing process itself, as the source of the internal constraint. Nonetheless we cannot completely account for a man's unfreedom simply because he was subjected to this process (external constraints). Consider: how would you decide when the effects of the brainwashing have been offset? The only situation in which they are completely offset, from the point of view of freedom, is when the ex-soldier's beliefs and actions are just what they would have been had he not been brainwashed. But how are we to tell when this goal has been achieved? It is not enough to work on him until his beliefs become identical to those he held prior to his brainwashing, for there is good reason to think that his beliefs would have undergone some changes simply with the passage of time. But since we do not know the direction these changes would have taken, trying to "unwash" the brain does not really make him free. It simply imposes a different set of beliefs than the enemy did. The only way a victim of brainwashing can be returned to a state of freedom is by restoring to him the beliefs he would now hold had he not been brainwashed.

Let's look at the familiar case of a person who compulsively washes his hands several hundred times a day (see this chapter, § Compatibilism). No external constraints force him to wash them; it is just that his hands always feel dirty to him. To say that there are no external constraints operative on him is not necessarily to deny that there is a cause for his action. Rather it is to point out that no one set about intentionally to turn this fellow into a compulsive handwasher. The only sense in which external factors are operative on him is the sense in which they are operative on everyone—viz., that people are tremendously influenced by what goes on around them.

It certainly seems that a compulsive handwasher does not wash his hands freely. But we cannot account for his compulsion or lack of freedom by tracing its source back to external constraints. As we have seen, the compulsive handwasher is no more nor less influenced by external constraints than anyone else. Hence if we want to say that the compulsive handwasher is unfree (and the noncompulsive free), as surely we do, we must say that there are certain internal constraints operative on the former but not on the latter, which account for the fact that the compulsive is unfree. Of course internal factors also operate on the noncompulsive, for clearly they do on everyone. The point here is that there is a special kind of internal factor (i.e. internal constraint) that renders compulsive acts unfree. Hence, the primary task for the advocate of positive freedom is to explain how internal constraints are different from other internal factors.

At this point, the trouble begins. Because of the way the advocates of positive freedom develop the notion of internal constraint, their concept of freedom comes into direct conflict with the concept of negative freedom. They take the view that sometimes it is necessary to impose external constraints in order to eliminate or offset internal constraints. In other words, for the advocates of positive freedom one can be free while acting under external constraint whereas for the advocates of negative freedom this is impossible. And thus there are points at which what the advocates of positive freedom call freedom the advocates of negative freedom call slavery (and vice versa).

### The Two Selves, Higher and Lower

To understand how the advocates of positive freedom end up with the conclusion that one can be free while acting under external constraint, we must look at the account they give of the self. All accounts of positive freedom begin with the idea that there are two selves--the higher, true, or real self and the lower or apparent self. One is free or internally *un*constrained when he acts according to his higher or real self and unfree or internally constrained when he acts according to his lower or apparent self. In other words, what renders our former P.O.W. unfree is that brainwashing involves the eclipsing of the true self by the apparent self, and what renders the compulsive unfree is that compulsive acts are acts of the lower self. Moreover, the way to make such people free is to restore the control of their thoughts and actions to the higher self (i.e. to unwash the brain and to eliminate the compulsion respectively).

You see by now how the distinction between higher and lower self allows the advocate of positive freedom to claim that in some instances the presence of external constraint is liberating and the absence of such constraint is enslaving. If we leave either the victim of brainwashing or the compulsive alone (i.e. impose no external constraints upon him) he is acting according to his lower self, and hence his actions are unfree. If, on the other hand, *we know how he would act if his actions were controlled by his higher self*, and we force him to act that way, then he is acting according to his higher self, and his actions are free.

Although all proponents of positive freedom agree on this much, they do not all agree when it comes to giving content to the notions of the higher and the lower self. The most popular view is that the higher self acts on the basis of reason and the lower on the basis of passion or appetite.[4] But one does not have to take this view. As we shall see in our discussion of fascism (ch. 7), sometimes the higher self is identified with the will of the ruler, and no attention at all is paid to whether this will is grounded in reason. One could even equate acting passionately with the higher self and acting rationally with the lower self if one wanted to.

However, because proponents of positive freedom usually associate acting rationally with the higher self, we examine this view in some detail. They believe that there are two sources of action—passion (or appetite) and reason. When one acts impulsively, the basis of desire, he is acting passionately. When, on the other hand, he scrutinizes his passions before acting upon them—when he deliberates about whether he should do something, and then does what he decides he should do—he is acting rationally. Since man is a rational animal (i.e. it is man's function to use his reason), free acts (i.e. acts of the higher self) are those based upon reason. When an act is the result of passion or impulse, on the other hand, it is unfree (i.e. an act of the lower self). In other words, when we act rationally we are truly ourselves, freely doing what we want to do; but when passion is the source of our actions we are not really in control of ourselves.

Think of someone on a diet, trying to lose ten pounds, and off to a good start. Suppose this person goes to visit a friend and unfortunatley gets seated right next to a dish of his favorite kind of candy. He starts to salivate, the desire for some candy grows and grows, while at the same time a voice within him (the voice of reason) cries out, "Don't eat the candy! Remember your diet!" His reason and his passion are in conflict.

As we have seen, acting passionately is identified with slavery and acting rationally with freedom. When a man gives in to his passions, he is being constrained by them, and is not acting freely. On the other hand, when he overcomes his passions and abides by his reason, he has liberated himself, and is acting freely. Moreover, when advocates of this view speak of following the dictates of reason, they mean reason in the strongest sense of the term. They come primarily from the rationalist tradition (Rousseau, Hegel, Marcuse, etc.), and believe that in every situation there is one course of action that is best, and that it is dictated by reason. On this there is no quibbling. Reason issues its commands to all people, and one merely needs to be rational to see what these commands are. What is right is right—universally, eternally, and incontrovertibly.[5]

What do these advocates of positive freedom do with the people who are not able to act rationally — with those who cannot see what reason requires, and those who can see what reason requires, but are constantly giving in to the promptings of their passions? They cannot be left alone (as the proponents of negative freedom advocate) for that would only ensure their continued enslavement. *The only way to free them is to force them to act in accordance with reason.* Perhaps at some point they will then act this way of their own accord. Until they do, however, their freedom consists in being forced to do what reason requires. And hence we arrive at a contradiction, at least the proponents of negative freedom insist that it is—viz., the idea that a person can be coerced and yet be free. For believers in negative freedom external constraints can only enslave; for the proponents of positive freedom external constraints are often necessary for liberation.

### How Adequate Is the Concept of Higher Self?

Aside from this conflict with negative freedom, the concept of positive freedom has other problems. Perhaps the most obvious and fundamental is a question that underlies its reasoning: How adequate is the conception of the higher self? Proponents maintain that an individual can be confused about what his higher self desires; if this were not possible, then it would make no sense to speak of forcing someone to be free. Further, the rationalist says that there is *a* rational course of action for every situation and that others may know what this course is even if the individual involved does not. But is there the kind of rational order that this view presupposes? If there is, how do we determine the content of that order? These problems came up in our discussion of dictatorial sovereignty; as indicated there, detailed consideration is postponed until our discussion of natural law (see ch. 4, § Natural Law and Rational Insight).

This same problem, albeit in a different form, arises on the nonrationalistic conception of positive freedom. In this view the desires of the higher self are equated with the will of the ruler. In other words, although an individual can be confused about what he *truly* desires, the ruler cannot be. But what reason is there to think that everyone really desires what the ruler says they desire? It would seem that if there is room for error, it is more likely that the ruler is mistaken about what his subjects desire than that they are mistaken about what they desire.

To make it plausible that acting freely and the higher self are connected, we must equate desiring with the higher self. It would be odd for someone to say, "I desire to go out but my mother won't let me, so my staying in is a free act." Certainly if you cannot do what you desire, then you are not free. But if being able to do what you desire is a **necessary condition** of being free and if to act freely is to act according to your higher self, then being able to do what you desire must also be a ncessary condition of acting according to your higher self. Thus, in our example of a dieter drooling over a dish of candy, we cannot say that he really desires the candy. Rather it must be that he really desires to diet even though he thinks that he desires the candy.

We all recognize that people do not always know what they desire. For example, a person simply may not be able to choose among a number of different alternatives open to him—he may be undecided as to which of the candidates for president he prefers. Or because of misinformation he may think he desires something that he really does not—he may favor one presidential candidate in the belief that he will cut taxes when in fact that candidate has no intention of doing so. And finally, it is also possible for someone not to know what he desires because he is not thinking rationally—he may think that cutting taxes is the only important issue and yet not favor the only candidate who advocates cutting them, somehow not recognizing the inconsistency of his position.

Thus there are at least three different ways in which a person may not know what he desires: (1) he has not made up his mind, (2) he has made up his mind without adequate information, and (3) he has made up his mind with adequate information but using faulty reasoning. But in the latter cases, if we are going to say that he does not know what he desires, then it must be that if what is lacking is supplied, he will change his mind accordingly. Once we have laid out for someone all the appropriate information and logical considerations and his desires still fly in the face of reason, we can no longer say, as the advocates of positive freedom do, that he does not know what he desires. He wants exactly what he thinks he wants, although his desires are irrational.

Another problem with the concept of positive freedom is that becuase of the difficulties involved in discerning what the higher self wills (assuming for the moment that there is a higher self), historically this conception of freedom has led to innumerable abuses. The catalogue of inhuman acts done to people in the name of their freedom is long and horrifying, and has led many to reject totally the concept of positive freedom. It is argued that as long as it is possible to do things *to* people in the name of freedom, the door is open to abuses. It is only by tying freedom to the absence of external constraints as the advocates of negative freedom propose, and thereby eliminating the possibility of forcing people to be free, that the justification of oppression in the name of freedom can be precluded. This of course does not prevent oppression from being justified in some other way. Nonetheless, to prevent the justification of oppression in the name of freedom is a significant accomplishment.[6]

### Positive and Negative Freedom: A Perspective

It should be clear that the source of each of these problems is the identification of acting freely with acting according to the higher self. Fortunately, however, there is a way of capturing the basic insight of the concept of positive freedom without creating these problems. We can take the view that acting according to the higher self (i.e. internally unconstrained) is a necessary condition of freedom, but it is not the sole and **sufficient condition**. This means that although one is not acting freely unless he is internally unconstrained, acting according to the higher self does not guarantee acting freely. This makes it possible to insist that the absence of external constraint is also a necessary condition of freedom; hence one is only free if he is both internally and externally unconstrained.

In other words, there is a difference between a person's doing something and a person's having something done to him—between commiting oneself to an institution for psychiatric treatment and being committed by others. Similarly there is a difference between acting according to your higher self and having someone force you to do what you would do if you were acting according to your higher self. Yet the advocates of positive freedom tend to lose sight of this distinction. For them you are free even if you are forced to do what you would do if you were acting according to your higher self. But I am arguing that it does make a difference, and that you are not free under such circumstances.

In other words, I am suggesting that, in order to be free, one must act in the absence of both external and internal constraints. This is not to deny that if one acts in the absence of external constraint but in the presence of internal constraint he is free in a sense—i.e. he is free from external constraint. Nor is it to deny that if he acts in the absence of internal constraint but in the presence of external constraint he is free in another sense—i.e. he is free from internal constraint. But neither of these senses of "freedom" constitute all there is to the concept. To be truly free one must be acting in the absence of both internal and external constraint.

The main advantage in this way of looking at the concepts of positive and negative freedom is to reinforce the idea that they are simply different components of the same concept. Such reinforcement is important because some thinkers speak as if the positive aspect (i.e. the absence of internal contraint) exhausts the concept of freedom, while others speak as if the negative aspect of freedom (i.e. the absence of external constraint) exhausts it. But neither of them do.

I have said that to be truly free a person must act in the absence of both internal and external constraints. But what about the person (the brainwashed P.O.W., the compulsive handwasher, etc.) who is the victim of internal constraint? If we leave him alone (i.e. leave him free from the external constraint), he will remain unfree from internal constraint. If, on the other hand, we force him to do those things he would do if he were free from internal constraint (assuming we know what these things are), then at the same time we make him free from internal constraint we enslave him to external constraint. What should we do with such a person? Should we leave him alone or force him to be (internally) free?

The answer one should give to this question may well be different in different cases. But a word of caution is in order: The imposition of external constraint to overcome internal constraint should only be resorted to, if at all, as a last resort. We have already seen the problems that arise when someone else claims to know better than the individual himself how he would act were it not for the internal constraint operative upon him. We have also seen how difficult it is to distinguish internal constraint from other kinds of internal factors that influence our thoughts and actions. And finally we have seen the kinds of abuses that have often accompanied the positive conception of freedom. In light of these problems, it would seem reasonable to adopt a very cautious attitude toward the idea that a person can be forced to be free.

In other words, I propose that we establish a strong presumption in favor of freedom in the negative sense of the absence of external constraint. If you believe that in a particular case someone should be externally constrained for the sake of overcoming internal constraint, you should have to argue for this view. And your argument should have to be sufficiently strong to outweigh the problems in the position you are taking. It may be that this argument can only be made successfully in the strongest of cases—the treatment of the mentally ill without their consent—or it may be that it cannot be successfully made in any case at all. But it seems reasonable that a very strong argument be required to support the claim that an individual be subjected to external constraint for the purpose of freeing him from internal constraint. And this is precisely what establishing a presumption in favor of the negative sense of freedom does.

### Freedom and Authority: An Assessment

Our analysis of the concept of freedom has revealed that the term *free* is used in a variety of different ways. With this analysis as background, we can make better sense of the ideas about freedom that we come across every day.

Whenever someone makes a claim about freedom, ask yourself, How is he using the term *freedom*? The content of his claim depends upon his use of this term, and we can only critically assess his claim when we understand what he means by it.

Further, this analysis has put us in a position to see and to appreciate the fundamental role that freedom plays in social and political thought. How and to what extent is it possible to live in society and yet be free? is the basic question. And from this arises a second, equally important question: If freedom is incompatible with a given form of sovereignty, is it still possible to justify that form of sovereignty?

Some thinkers insist that freedom and authority are incompatible—that it is impossible to live under the authority of others and yet be free. Of these, the anarchist concludes that authority is never justified. He advocates individual sovereignty because he believes that it is the only form of sovereignty compatible with freedom. This conclusion only follows because he also believes that freedom is more important than whatever advantages result from living under an established authority. Other thinkers, although agreeing with the anarchist that freedom and authority are incompatible, reject the conclusion that the exercise of power cannot be justified. They argue that the loss in freedom associated with authority is outweighed by the tremendous cultural and material advantages that result from its establishment.

In contrast, others claim that freedom and authority are compatible. This position is argued for in two different ways. As we have seen, in the positive conception, freedom is compatible with coercion. Those thinkers who equate the higher self with the duly constituted authority (either directly—the higher self wills whatever the ruler wills—or indirectly—the higher self wills what is rational and the ruler is the only one who knows what is rational) conclude that people are free when they are following the dictates of the duly constituted authority; and hence freedom and authority are perfectly compatible.

The other attempt to reconcile freedom and authority employs the concept of negative freedom. Utilizing the paradox of freedom (all freedom is purchased at the expense of freedom) it is argued that the sacrifice of freedom associated with the establishment of authority is necessary for securing freedom. In the absence of authority, people are always infringing upon the freedom of others, and hence an established authority is necessary for freedom to exist effectively (as opposed to merely formally).

And so we are ready, in the chapters that follow, to address the question: What justifies some individuals or groups having authority over others? We do not again directly discuss the view that such authority cannot be justified (i.e. anarchism) nor do we discuss the answer proposed by the advocates of positive freedom. Rather we focus on the claims that authority is justified by the increase in either the effective freedom or the human welfare it provides. However, our answers have implications for the positions taken by both the anarchist and the proponent of positive freedom; and hence it is important for you to keep these positions in mind.

## NOTES

1. I prefer the term *free choice* to *free will* and use it throughout.

2. For a discussion which rejects the view that the best way to understand the sociopolitical concept of freedom is by means of the distinction between positive and negative freedom, see Gerald C. MacCallum, Jr., "Negative and Positive Freedom," *Philosophical Review,* 76 (July 1967): 312-34.

3. John Stuart Mill, *On Liberty* (Indianapolis: Bobbs-Merrill, 1956), p. 13.

4. Thus, Rousseau says, "for it is *slavery* to be under the impulse of mere appetite, and *freedom* to obey a law we prescribe for ourselves (i.e. act rationally)." See Jean Jacques Rousseau, *The Social Contract,* rev. and ed. by Charles Frankel (New York: Hafner Publishing Company, 1947), p. 19.

5. It is interesting that the advocates of negative freedom tend to come from the empiricist tradition (Hobbes, Locke, Mill, etc.). As such they are much less dogmatic about what is right and are far more willing to let people alone to decide what they think is right.

6. For a more detailed development of this line of argument see Isaiah Berlin, "Two Concepts of Liberty," in *Four Essays on Liberty*, Isaiah Berlin (London: Oxford University Press, 1969), pp. 118-72, and Gerald C. MacCallum, Jr., "Negative and Positive Freedom," *Philosophical Review,* 76 (July 1967): 312-34.

# 4

## The Social Contract, Rule of Law, and Natural Rights

One of the most frequent answers to the question, What justifies living under the authority of others? is that only by the establishment of an authority can the rights that individuals naturally possess be guaranteed. In the vernacular of freedom, this answer says that people are only effectively free when their rights are respected by others, and only by the establishment of authority can such respect be assured. In order to provide the background necessary for understanding and appreciating the significance of this answer, we begin by looking at the concepts of the social contract and the rule of law.

### THE SOCIAL CONTRACT

The social contract is an agreement that sets up an authority for governing; it establishes the right to power. Social contract theories hence attempt to answer the question, What justifies some people having authority over others? They also present a conception of the form this authority should take. To accomplish these ends, three main concepts are employed: (1) the idea of an original situation (the state of nature), (2) an agreement (the social contract among those in this original situation), and finally, (3) a new and better way of living (civil society). In the state of nature individual sovereignty prevails and hence no one has authority over anyone else. The social contract sets up a duly constituted authority (i.e. establishes either a dictator or the people as sovereign) and a government through which this authority can be effected. Civil society is life under that duly constituted authority and government machinery. Social contract theories argue that life in civil society is better than life in the state of nature, but that the only way to live in society is by recognizing an authority.

Although at times social contract theorists sound as if they are presenting descriptive theories, it is not their intention to do so. They do not think that at one time people actually lived in a state of nature, then they came together and signed a contract, and from that time on lived in civil society. Rather, they say that the state of nature would exist if people did not live as if there were a social contract. And because the state of nature is so undesirable, living as if there were a social contract (with whatever sacrifice of freedom this entails) is justified. In other words, the ideas of the state of nature and the social contract are intended as hypothetical constructs.

Second, although all social contract theorists utilize the same three concepts—state of nature, social contract, and civil society—their theories differ widely in detail. To illustrate both the nature and the scope of these differences we shall examine the theories of Thomas Hobbes and John Locke. Do not infer that, because these are the only two we examine, they are the only forms of the theory; they are simply two of the more interesting, important, and representative versions.

### Hobbes: All Give Authority to One

According to Hobbes, the state of nature is dog-eat-dog chaos. There is no cooperation among individuals; everyone is in constant fear that everything he has (including his life) will be taken by another. In this state of constant conflict, individuals do whatever is necessary to get what they want, and "the life of man (is) solitary, poor, nasty, brutish, and short."[1] It is a very undesirable way to live.

The trouble with the state of nature is that the individual is completely sovereign. There is no ruler to lay down the law and force individuals to obey. Hence, when the desires of individuals conflict, there is bound to be difficulty. The only alternative, according to Hobbes, is to put absolute power in the hands of one man or an assembly of men. This vesting of power is expressed by the social contract, which authorizes all the actions of the ruler.

This is more than consent or concord; it is a real unity of them all in one and the same person, made by covenant of every man with every man, in such a manner as if every man should say to every man, *I authorize and give up my right of governing myself to this man, or to this assembly of men, on this condition, that you give up your right to him and authorize all his actions in a like manner.*[2]

Notice first in this contract that sovereignty is being transferred from all individuals to one man (or an assembly of men). Hence the giving up of individual sovereignty must be justified. And Hobbes believes that it is justified by the fact that, as long as there is individual sovereignty, there will be chaos and complete insecurity. Notice also that this transfer of sovereignty from individuals to one man is both irreversible and absolute. It must be irreversible because, if individuals can take their authority back, then sovereignty still rests in their hands; hence chaos and insecurity have not been eliminated. It must be absolute because, as long as any authority whatsoever remains in the hands of individuals, the kind of conflict that is the hallmark of the state of nature will still exist.

For these reasons the social contract, as Hobbes formulates it, is between the individuals themselves rather than between the individuals and the ruler. Each individual agrees to transfer his sovereignty to one man or an assembly of men not on the condition that that man do certain things, but only on the condition that everyone else transfer their sovereignty as well. By making the ruler the beneficiary of the contract rather than a party to it, Hobbes allows for his complete sovereignty. Because the sovereign does not agree to anything in becoming the ruler, his authority is not limited in any way.

### Locke: All Agree to Abide by Majority Rule

John Locke's social contract theory is very different from Hobbes's. Whereas Hobbes views the state of nature as a situation in which there is no society (at least as we have defined the term) because there is no cooperation at all among the individuals, to Locke in the state of nature there is cooperation. It is not complete chaos and confusion, but rather a situation in which people work pretty well together. The state of nature is governed by the laws of nature—those principles, discoverable by reason, which embody respect for the lives and happiness of others. The only real problem is that, given individual sovereignty, there is no way to enforce the laws of nature—i.e. no way of promulgating them and punishing violators. Each individual must decide what the laws of nature are and whether or not he will follow them. And the only way to rectify violation of the laws of nature is by taking retaliatory action oneself. Although this does not totally destroy the harmony between people, it does create problems. And the solution to these problems is the establishment of an authority who can promulgate and enforce the laws of nature as laws of the land.

For Locke, the social contract is an agreement to abide by majority rule (i.e. it is the substitution of popular for individual sovereignty). Its main function is to allow for the enactment and enforcement of the laws of nature. It replaces the rule of individual judgment and fancy characteristic of the state of nature by the rule of clearly formulated and promulgated laws. By punishing those who violate the laws and thus discouraging lawbreakers, it provides as much protection as possible from the interference of others. In short, Locke's theory does not replace chaos with order as Hobbes's does; rather, for Locke, the social contract simply gives a formal basis to the cooperative efforts in which men are always involved. It provides the security of knowing that those who do not cooperate with the laws of nature (which have become the laws of the land) will be punished.

Hobbes and Locke use the same basic elements to provide radically different theories. This fact becomes all the more interesting when you realize that both were Englishmen and that the works in which their social contract theories appear were published only 39 years apart—Hobbes's *Leviathan,* 1651; Locke's *Second Treatise on Government,* 1690. Yet these differences are not surprising when you consider the setting in which they lived and their purposes in developing their theories. In their day, the doctrine of the divine right of kings was under attack, and there was a continual struggle for power between the king and the Parliament. Hobbes wanted to see the sovereignty of the monarch preserved, and yet he doubted that the divine right of kings was a tenable doctrine. Hence he sought a way to justify the authority of the monarch (dictatorial sovereignty) without employing the theory of the divine right. So he attempted to base the sovereignty of the monarch on the initial sovereignty of the individual by showing why individuals should completely and irrevocably transfer their sovereignty to one man.

Locke also rejected the divine right of kings and, along with it, the idea of the sovereignty of the monarch. However he wrote in defense of the bloodless revolution of 1688—which reaffirmed Parliament's dominance over the king. Hence his concern was to establish the principle of majoritarian (representative) rule, and he spun the elements of social contract theory into a web to serve this purpose.

However, we are not primarily concerned with the question, What motivated Hobbes and Locke to develop their theories in diverse directions? Rather our concern is, How is it logically possible for Hobbes and Locke to use the same elements of social contract theory and yet argue in such radically different directions? The answer is, because they begin their arguments from very different conceptions of human nature.

### *Hobbes and Locke: There is an Unchangeable Human Nature*

Hobbes believed that all human beings are egoistic, that each individual will do whatever is necessary to promote his own self-interest. If you have something I want, and I feel that I can get it away from you, I will try to take it. If we agree to do something, and you do your part but I do not feel like doing mine or I see that it is not in my interest to do so, then I will not keep the bargain. Because people are this way, and recognize that everyone else is, they will not take the risk of cooperative endeavors. They are unwilling to do their share without the assurance that others will do theirs.

In short, people will work together and keep the agreements they make only if a power over them forces them to—i.e. someone punishes them if they do not cooperate. In the state of nature there is no such power because men are basically equal in strength and cunning. But the social contract establishes such a power. The sovereign rules through a reign of terror, forcing people to do his will at the threat of imprisonment or death. In short, Hobbes believes that, given man's nature, social cooperation can exist only when it is forced on the people by an absolute ruler. And it is in the interest of everyone to establish such a ruler because he offers the only possible way to get out of the state of nature, and nothing is worse than life in the state of nature.

Whereas Hobbes believes that human beings are egoistic, Locke feels that people can and do look beyond their own interests. They generally recognize that it is not *their* life, *their* happiness, *their* property that is of value but rather life, happiness, property per se, no matter whose they are. In other words, people generally realize that everyone has these rights and more often than not honor them. Thus even in the original situation, because of man's basic nature, there is the respect for others necessary for cooperation. That life, happiness, and property are valuable is, for Locke, a matter of natural law; it is discoverable by reason which is present in everyone. Of course, people do not always use their reason to discover these laws nor do they always obey their reason once they have discovered them, and this is precisely why civil society is an improvement over the state of nature. Nevertheless in the state of nature people use and follow reason enough to make cooperation and harmony possible.

It should be clear that the basic disagreement between Hobbes and Locke involves man's nature. If Hobbes's assessment is correct, Locke's system of majority rule cannot work, for it does not allow for a ruler to club people into cooperating. If, on the other hand, Locke's account of human nature is correct, then there is no need for such clubbing; people can get along fine under majority rule. Although there may be reasons for rejecting majority rule, that it cannot work is not one.

### Human Nature: Unchangeable? Does It Exist?

However, there is another perspective from which to view the dispute between Hobbes and Locke. Although it never occurred to either of them to doubt that human nature is fixed and unchangeable, people have done so during the last two hundred years. With the development of the medical and social sciences, scholars have begun to empirically investigate human behavior. As the social, psychological, and physical behavior of human beings has been studied closely, more and more people have come to believe that human nature is changeable.

Many today believe that, although much of what we are is largely a result of heredity (i.e. our genetic endowment), there is no set genetic endowment that everyone is born with; there are as many different "human natures" as there are possible genetic arrangements. Some go to the extreme of saying that there is no such thing as human nature. B. F. Skinner, probably the most famous proponent of this view, believes that our behavior and ideas are entirely a product of the environment.[3] In short, we are what we have been conditioned to be.

This dispute over whether or not there is a fixed and unchanging human nature underlies some of the controversy between capitalism and communism. Many defenders of capitalism insist that communism can never work because profit is the basic determinant of human behavior, and communism requires people to work without that motivation. Opposed to this view of a fixed and unalterable human nature, proponents of communism argue that if profit motivates human behavior, it is only because people have been conditioned this way. In other words, all that the existence of the profit motive shows is that people will have to be "prepared" (i.e. reconditioned ) to live under communism, not that they cannot live under such a system.

All these arguments about the qualities of human nature are less fundamental than the question, Is there such a thing as human nature? If it is determined that there is no such thing as human nature, then the accounts of Hobbes and Locke as well as the defense of capitalism based upon an unchanging human nature, must be rejected out of hand. If, on the other hand, it is determined that there is such a thing as human nature, then we must consider which view accurately describes that nature.

No matter how one resolves this issue, one must address the basic normative concern, What is the best form for life to take? Hobbes and Locke believed that there is a human nature and set out to try to discover the best possible form of life, given that nature. If one accepts the view that there is no human nature— that either through genetic engineering or operant conditioning (or both) we can make people into whatever we want them to be—then we still must consider whether or not (and if so to what end) "human engineering" should be used. Hence in either view of human nature we must come to grips with the basic normative issue of what form of life we should strive to effect.

### Why Should Some People Have Authority Over Others?

In addition to the dispute over man's basic nature, two other issues are raised by the social contract theories of Hobbes and Locke. Even granting his account of human nature, Hobbes must still show that people are better off living under the hand of an absolute ruler than in the state of nature. He attempts to do this by painting such a grim picture of the state of nature that almost anything would be an improvement. But at least in the state of nature one can compete with one's peers on a roughly equal basis. In civil society, on the other hand, there is a ruler against whom one is powerless. Is one really better off living under the hand of such a powerful man who can do anything he wants to?

On the other hand, Locke must show that people are better off living under majority rule than if each retained his individual sovereignty. This task is of course complicated because Locke sees the state of nature as a situation where cooperation is the rule rather than the exception. Hence he must show in what way popular sovereignty is an improvement on individual sovereignty.

We are in effect back where we began. The basic question of social and political thought is, Why should some people have authority over others? Social contract theorists agree that human beings are better off living under an authority than living without one. They provide a hypothetical construct, the social contract, to represent the replacement of individual by either dictatorial or popular sovereignty. But this construct does not, by itself, show that such a replacement is desirable. It must still be argued that living under an authority is preferable to living without one. The advantages and disadvantages of living under a duly constituted authority must still be examined and evaluated. Although we do this against the backdrop of social contract theory, these questions arise for anyone concerned with justifying the existence of power, and are paramount in today's world.

## THE RULE OF LAW

One of the main advantages of civil society is the rule of law. This rule removes much insecurity that is the hallmark of the state of nature. Without the paraphernalia of law, each person is entirely at the mercy of others. There are no set rules to govern behavior, no judges to decide when the rules have been violated, no penal system to punish offenders. Everyone must stand up for himself, protect himself as best he can, and of his own accord seek restitution for wrongs done to him.

The implementation of the rule of law changes all this. Individuals can no longer live simply by whim or by rules of their own making. A legislature is set up and charged with the responsibility of deciding on the rules by which the society shall be governed, a judiciary with adjudicating all purported violations of the law, and finally an executive with enforcing the law. It does not matter whether these functions are performed by different bodies under the doctrine of "the separation of powers" or whether they all rest in the hands of the same body or individual. The point is that these functions must be performed in order for people to live under the rule of law. In short, the rule of law presupposes the existence of at least some formal structure of government.

The rule of law must have certain formal characteristics. Some thinkers[4] insist that if these characteristics are not present then the rules, even if enacted by a duly constituted legislature, are not really laws. Others make the weaker claim that these are the characteristics that *good* laws must have. We are concerned about these formal characteristics because they indicate how the rule of law provides security absent from the state of nature.

### Formal Characteristics of the Rule of Law

The first condition of the rule of law is that rules must be formulated. This may at first sound silly. After all, what is a law other than a rule? But it is not silly at all. What it points to is the crucial difference between governance by established rules and by arbitrary decrees. Under arbitrary decrees a person can be punished at any time for anything he does, depending upon the whims of those who make and enforce the law. But under the law there is a set of rules which lay down what may and may not be done, what punishments are appropriate to what offenses.

Another characteristic is that rules must be understandable and well publicized. They must not be retroactive (apply to acts performed before the law was enacted) if this will result in harm to those who acted in good faith. Nor can they be contradictory. If these conditions are not met, it is impossible to know what the law is and how to avoid violating it. But with the establishment of laws that meet these conditions, people are well on their way to living in a secure environment. They know what they must do to avoid punishment, and they also know that others will be punished if they violate the law.

Further, the rule of law requires an impartial, objective, and consistent judicial system which adjudicates purported violations of the law. Judicial decisions must not favor any individual or group of individuals; they must attempt to apply the law as it is written, not according to esoteric interpretations beyond the understanding of the citizens; the same act cannot be required by one law and prohibited by another. If these conditions are not met, individuals cannot know how they must behave in order to avoid running afoul of judicial decisions.

Finally there must be an executive to enforce the law. From the setting down of riots to the bringing of charges against those who violate the law, executives should act in a fair and impartial way. There should not be different standards of enforcement for different groups. Everyone should be given the same treatment and should be kept in line to the same degree by the law.

If the laws apply to everyone equally, then under the rule of law every individual can at least be satisfied that he is being treated fairly vis-à-vis his peers. Everyone is subject to the same laws; enforcement is done in an evenhanded way; when punishment is involved, those committing the same crime are given the same punishment. At least in this way no one gains the upper hand over another through the implementation of the rule of law. Indeed, why should anyone give up individual sovereignty to live under a system of law which favors others and works to his own disadvantage?

If one is going to reject individual sovereignty, it seems that the establishment of the rule of law, as described here, is a necessary condition for doing so. But it is not a sufficient condition. More is needed to justify a system of dictatorial or popular sovereignty instead of individual sovereignty. Why? Because the fair enactment, adjudication, and enforcement of laws is compatible with the most horrendous laws imaginable. It is compatible with a law that prescribes the death penalty for those who sneeze in public, with a law that allows wiretapping and forceful entry for any reason whatsoever, and with a law that prohibits sexual intercourse except under certain circumstances and in prescribed ways. As long as such laws are formulated in such a way that they apply to everyone, are enforced evenhandedly and adjudicated fairly, the minimum conditions of the rule of law have been met. Yet surely these laws do not make it desirable to live under the authority of either a dictator or the people.

The rule of law merely sets down formal conditions that laws must meet. Because both good and bad laws can meet these conditions, there is a need for more than these formal conditions. There must be a way of restricting the content as well as the form of law, of making sure that laws also guarantee that life in civil society will be desirable.


## WHAT ARE RIGHTS?

One way of giving content to the law is by developing a theory of natural rights or natural law. The basic idea is that there are certain rights that all individuals naturally have.[5] The establishment and protection of these rights should be the primary function of the rule of law. However, we cannot examine the theory of natural rights until we know more about what a right is.

Perhaps the best way to explain the notion of a right is to look at one—the right to property. What is the difference between property and a possession? To possess something is to have it under your control. If someone else takes it from you, then he possesses it. There is no sense in which your possession can be violated, for the term *possession* merely describes whose control a given item is under. To have property, however, is quite different. It involves having a legitimate claim to a given item. And to have a legitimate claim means that other people should recognize your claim and respect the item as yours. If you leave it unguarded, they should not take it. If you lose it and someone finds it, he should return it to you. Thus, whenever a mere possession is taken from you, it ceases to be yours and becomes the possession of another. But when your property is taken from you, although it has become the possession of another, it is still your property. And it remains your property either until you renounce your claim to it or the person who has taken it from you can establish a claim to it that overrides yours.

There is, then, a connection between the idea of a right and of a duty or obligation. In most cases, a right entails the obligation on the part of others to allow an individual to exercise that right. The right to property entails the obligation on the part of others not to take possessions. The right to free speech entails the obligation on the part of others not to restrict speech. The right to a fair trial entails the obligation on the part of others not to interfere with or subvert due process of law. And so on. But even though having a right entails other people's having obligations, it imposes no obligations on the person who has the right. In this regard having a right is like having the permission to do something rather than like having the duty to do it. You may exercise the right if you want to, but you are not obligated to exercise it. Of course you may have both the right and the duty to do the same thing. But if you do, the right and the duty are distinct. You cannot have the duty simply because you have the right.

For example, to say that someone has a right to life entails that everyone else has a duty not to take his life.[6] Thus the claim that a fetus has a right to life entails that abortion violates the rights of the fetus. But the right to life cannot be used as an argument against suicide. The committing of suicide is not a violation of the right to life; it is merely the decision on the part of an individual no longer to exercise his right to life. Thus if you want to argue that suicide is wrong, you must argue either in terms of the individual's obligation to remain alive (e.g. he has a responsibility to his family) or in terms of the individual's *not* having the right to take his own life (e.g. God gives life and only He has the right to take it). But you cannot argue that suicide is wrong because it violates the right to life. To be wrong it must violate the duty or obligation to life, not the right.

### Which Right Should Take Precedence?

Any theory of rights must come to grips with the basic problem of how to resolve conflicts among rights. Because these conflicts arise so frequently, a theory that fails to resolve them is totally inadequate as a guide to action. The conflicts can be either intra- or transcategorial in nature. An intracategorial conflict involves two claims to the same right, which cannot both be satisfied. These conflicts clearly arise in times of scarcity. Thus, when there is not enough food to go around, everyone's right to life is threatened. Whose right should take precedence? Who should have the first claim to the food that is available? The weak who will be the first to die when food is short? The strong who have the best chance of surviving? Or the wealthy who can pay the most for whatever food is available?

Intracategorial conflicts also arise during times of abundance when two individuals want to exercise the same right in the same place at the same time. Suppose, for example, two people are walking toward each other on a collision course. Which one has the right to continue on course and which one should defer? How do we decide whose right to walk down the street (or right to liberty) takes precedence?

Transcategorial conflicts, on the other hand, involve conflicts between two different kinds of rights, rather than between the claims of different individuals to the same right. When a chain smoker comes in contact with a nonsmoker who is made uncomfortable by the smell of smoke, which one should defer to the other? Should the smoker's right to smoke take precedence over the non-smoker's right to comfort, or vice versa? One can attempt to resolve such conflicts either in general terms by establishing a rule to the effect that a given right always takes precedence over another right, or by deciding each particular case on its own merits. But either way the rights are given, and the task is to decide which is the most important.

When it comes to intracategorial conflicts, on the other hand, it is not a question of trying to decide which of two rights is the most important. There is only one right, and the question is, Whose right to it should be violated and whose preserved? There are no easy cases in which one right is obviously less important than the other, because the rights themselves are not in conflict. It is individuals who are in conflict, and what must be decided is which individual is the most important. For this reason, although transcategorial conflicts are the most prevalent, intracategorial conflicts are the most perplexing.

## THE THEORY OF NATURAL RIGHTS

### Natural and Conventional Rights

We are now close to understanding how the theory of natural rights can be presented in concert with the rule of law in an attempt to justify living under a system of law. In order to see how this can be done, one more distinction must be drawn—that between natural and conventional rights (or laws). Conventional rights, as the term *convention* suggests, are the product of agreement or compact between persons. Such rights are established by an agreement either directly, as when a group of people come together, or indirectly, as when a group of people authorize an individual or a group to establish rights. Because conventional rights are the creation of people, they are subject to change by those who create them.

Natural rights, on the other hand, are not the product of an agreement or compact between persons. Rather they are part of the natural order. In other words, just as a person has a heart, lungs, and kidneys, so too he has natural rights. These rights are inalienable. Because they are not the creation of persons, they cannot be given up or taken away by others. Of course, they can be ignored. We simply point out here that people have them whether or not they are recognized, respected, or embodied in conventions.

Proponents of the theory of natural rights have different views concerning how we know the laws which state these rights. During the Middles Ages, the theory of natural rights was understood primarily in theological terms. The natural law which should govern man's behavior was God's law, and it could be discovered by studying His revealed word. But there were some thinkers, most notably St. Thomas Aquinas (1225-1274), who believed that these laws were also discoverable by the use of reason. By the Seventeenth and Eighteenth centuries, the theological aspects had pretty much disappeared, and natural law was understood primarily as discoverable by the use of reason alone.

### Why Are Rights "Natural"?

Because, proponents of this view tell us, there is an objective moral order in the universe. There are certain rules that ought to govern human behavior, certain acts that are right and certain acts that are wrong: this rightness and wrongness exists objectively as part of the natural world. In this regard moral laws have the same status as the physical laws of motion, gravity, etc. They are not mere constructs of a human mind, but in some sense actually exist in the external world. They are eternal and unchanging. Of course we cannot observe the moral laws at work in the same way that we can observe the physical. After all, moral laws tell us what people ought to do rather than what they in fact do. If morality were concerned with how people do in fact behave, we would not have any problem. But moral laws are normative rather than descriptive, and so they cannot be empirically observed. Thus there is a crucial difference between the moral and the physical laws of nature—a difference so important that it may render the analogy between the two useless.

But the proponents of natural law are well aware that the moral laws are not empirically observable. Their point is merely that moral laws are as real as physical laws, not that they are learned in the same way. The proper method for discovering the moral laws of nature is reason rather than observation. Hence, with regard to their method of discovery, moral laws are more like the principles of mathematics and logic than they are like the physical laws. In other words, the moral laws of nature are a mixed bag, and because of this natural law theory can be approached from two very different perspectives.

The metaphysician attempts to determine whether or not moral and physical laws really do exist in the same way. If they do, how can we describe this form of existence? If they do not, in what sense do moral laws exist? Because of the complexity, however, we shall only mention this range of problems.

### Natural Law and Rational Insight

The epistemologist, on the other hand, attempts to determine the extent to which and the sense in which we can have knowledge of moral laws. To make the claim that there are such laws is very different from saying that we can have knowledge of them. The proponents of natural-law theory claim that we gain knowledge of these laws in the same way that we gain knowledge of the principles of mathematics and logic—through rational insight. But is this really the case?

There are two different senses in which the principles of mathematics and logic are known through rational insight. First, it is impossible to conceive of what it would be like for certain principles to be false (i.e. their falsity involves a contradiction). Consider the claim, There can be no such thing as a round square. Given what the terms *round* and *square* mean, it is impossible to even conceive that something could be both. Hence there is more to the claim that the principle There can be no such thing as a round square is known through rational insight than the mere fact that all rational beings accept the principle.

The reason that this principle is accepted by all rational beings is the impossibility of conceiving of what a round square would be like.

To justify the claim that there is a natural right to life in this sense, one would have to argue that given the concepts *human being* and *right to life*, it is impossible to conceive of a human being without the right to life. But it certainly is possible to conceive of a human being not having the right to life (and any other right for that matter); and hence the epistemological status of natural laws cannot be the same as the epistemological status of the principle There can be no such thing as a round square.

There are other principles that are self-evident, and therefore true, in spite of the fact that it is possible to conceive of them being false.

This reasoning is weak. Consider, for example, the principle Equals plus equals gives equals. It certainly is possible to conceive of what it would be like for this principle to be false. For example, combining one cup of alcohol with one cup of water yield less than two cups of liquid. And yet everyone capable of rational thought "sees" that equals plus equals gives equals—i.e. the principle is self-evident.

For the natural laws of morality to have the same epistemological status as this kind of principle, they must be self-evident. Thus, to show that the right to life is rational in this sense, one must prove it is self-evident that all human beings have this right. The only test that a principle is self-evident is that all rational beings "see" it to be true. Throughout history there have been numerous seemingly rational individuals who have not "seen" that there is a right to life; and countless others who, seeing that there is such a right, have disagreed about its nature. Therefore, the right to life, or any other purported natural right, does not pass the test.

If one denies the right to life, he is in effect saying that the necessary connection between being human and having the right to life is not self-evident. This view has been most widely held by fascist thinkers (see ch. 7, § Fascism). The mere existence of such a view among a significant number of people creates problems for those who claim that the principles of natural law are self-evident. They must either argue that all these individuals are irrational—a very difficult task indeed in light of the fact that most of them seem to be rational in every other respect (see ch. 6, § Paternalism)—or else they must give up the claim that the principles of natural law are self-evident.

Even those who believe that there is a right to life, however, disagree considerably over its nature. Can the right to life be forfeited? Some believe that it can and others believe that it cannot. Let's consider the dispute over capital punishment. Some thinkers maintain that putting a person to death for certain offenses is not a violation of the right to life because those who commit such offenses forfeit their right to life. Opponents, on the other hand, argue that the right to life cannot be forfeited, and hence capital punishment is a violation of this right.

Those who accept the theory of natural rights also disagree on how to resolve intra- and transcategorial conflicts of rights. When two rights conflict, or when the same right of different individuals conflict, which right or which individual's right take precedence? We have already discussed the problems involved in attempting to resolve such conflicts (see this ch., § Which Right Should Take Precedence?) and it seems fair to say that there are no self-evident solutions. Rational beings, even should they agree on the existence of a set of natural rights, will disagree considerably about resolving the conflicts that arise between these rights.

### Conclusions about the Theory of Natural Rights

Thus we are faced with the following situation. The claim that there are natural rights or laws is the claim that there are self-evident moral principles. The only test for these principles is that all rational beings "see" their truth. However, no moral principles seem to satisfy this requirement. When it comes to even the least controversial of the purported natural rights (e.g. the right to life) there is considerably more disagreement than one might suppose. Many of those who accept the idea that such rights are natural disagree about their substantive application—they disagree about whether these rights can be forfeited and about how to resolve conflicts between them. Furthermore, there is also a significant number of seemingly rational individuals who simply deny the existence of such rights.

It seems necessary, therefore, to reject the idea that conventional rights should be assessed in terms of natural rights. Even if there are natural laws, there seems to be no way to determine what these laws are. This conclusion leads some thinkers to take the position called normative skepticism (see ch. 1, § normative skepticism). They believe that natural law is the only adequate normative test of conventional law; hence, if knowledge of natural law is unattainable, there is no normative standard for conventional law. In other words, such law is simply the creation of the sovereign. They conclude that although it is possible to answer the procedural questions of whether the sovereign has the authority (however this may be defined) to enact a given law and whether the sovereign followed established procedures (whatever these may be) in enacting a particular law, it is not possible to answer the question, Is that law morally good or bad?

But many thinkers who believe that natural law is an unacceptable theory do not embrace normative skepticism. They insist that there is an answer to the question, What should be the content of conventional law? They believe that the justification for living under the authority of others is that the welfare of all people is served; hence, conventional law should be judged in terms of how well or poorly this end is achieved. This position is taken by the utilitarian, and we examine it in detail in the next chapter.

*NOTES*

1. Thomas Hobbes, *Leviathan* (New York: Bobbs-Merrill, 1958), p. 107.

2. Hobbes, *Leviathan*, p. 142.

3. See B. F. Skinner, *Beyond Freedom and Dignity* (New York: Alfred A. Knopf, 1972).

4. See Lon L. Fuller, *The Morality of Law* (New Haven, Connecticut: Yale University Press, 1964), ch. 2.

5. Sometimes referred to as "human rights," because all people possess them by virtue of the fact that they are human.

6. Whether or not it also entails that other people must take actions to save his life raises a host of issues that we need not go into.

# 5
## *Utilitarianism and Justice*

We have been discussing the questions, What justifies living under the authority of the state? and What should the content of the law be? As you recall, proponents of the theory of rights insist that the basic purpose of living under a duly constituted authority and of having rules to govern our behavior (i.e. the law) is to guarantee the rights that naturally belong to all human beings; once these rights are guaranteed, they believe, cooperative activity will emerge. Utilitarians, on the other hand, declare that the primary purpose of cooperative activity is to maximize human welfare, and hence the establishing of an authority and the enacting of rules should facilitate this end. In other words, the utilitarian rejects the idea that there are natural rights and proposes the principle of utility as the standard by which to judge both the establishment of authority and the content of law.

## *UTILITARIANISM*

Applied to the rules or laws of society, the principle of utility (known as rule-utilitarianism), requires that laws should maximize the general good or the general welfare of the society. In other words, it functions as a general criterion by which to assess all prospective laws. Only if they maximize the general welfare should they be passed. Perhaps you are already familiar with the principle of utility as applied to particular acts. In this form, known as act-utilitarianism, the principle requires that one perform the particular acts that maximize the general welfare.

### *Cooperation*

To clarify the differences between the theory of rights and utilitarianism as applied to the rule of law, the principle of utility must be examined in some detail. To understand it, we look at an underlying idea, cooperation. One can think of cooperation in terms of three main purposes it may have: (1) protection against the forces of nature, (2) provision for the necessities of life, (3) improvement of the standard of living.

One of the obvious advantages of social living is protection against the forces of nature. People respond to nature's challenges far more effectively in groups than as individuals. Be it a flood, an earthquake, or attacks by wild animals, the more hands that cooperate in defense against the devastation, the better are the chances for survival.

But there is also strength in numbers when it comes to providing the necessities of life—food, clothing, and shelter. Nature often attacks these rather than human life. And through cooperation the production of the necessities can be made to increase geometrically rather than arithmetically. In other words, if two men simply produced twice the amount of food that one man can (an arithmetic progression), then the only advantage to be gained from cooperation would be protection against the forces of nature. But by dividing the labor and sharing the tools, two men can hunt, fish, farm, and build far more effectively than either could do alone. Through cooperation more can be produced at less of a cost.

Of course the advantages of cooperative activity do not stop with the necessities. Indeed some would insist that the real advantages begin where the necessity for survival ends. For through cooperative activity alone can human beings produce and enjoy the niceties of life. Only through the division of labor and the development of technology can an economy provide the luxuries of material comfort and cultural development.

The purposes of cooperative activity, then, fall into two main categories: on the one hand, the demands of survival, composed of both the need for protection against the forces of nature and provision for the necessities of life; on the other hand, raising the level of life to the highest plane possible. Yet when the utilitarian speaks of maximizing the general good or the general welfare, he usually has in mind something more fundamental than either.

### Hedonism and the Utilitarian

Most utilitarians are hedonists. A hedonist believes that happiness or pleasure is the *only* thing that is good in itself. In this view, wealth is valuable only as a means to happiness; a work of art derives its value from the happiness that comes to those who view it; and most important, social goods such as rights and freedom only have value insofar as they bring happiness to those who possess them. Should certain rights or certain freedoms make people less happy than they might otherwise be, then such rights and freedoms should not exist. For the hedonist, there are no natural rights.

Although most utilitarians are hedonists, not all of them are. Some utilitarians believe that happiness is only a part of the good. Such a utilitarian might believe that in addition to happiness, beauty is valuable in itself; therefore, a work of art has value even if no one derives pleasure or happiness from looking at it. Or he might believe that a person's freedom is a good, regardless of whether or not that freedom is a source of happiness.

The basic problem that faces the utilitarian is to develop, and then to defend, an adequate account of the good or welfare. If he accepts hedonism, he must give an account of the nature of happiness. What is it? How can it be measured? What is the relationship between it and pleasure? And so on. If, on the other hand, he rejects hedonism, his task is even more difficult. Not only must he give an account of the nature of happiness, he must also explain his other values (e.g. freedom) and what to do when values conflict with each other—e.g. What should one do when freedom makes people unhappy?

Difficult as these problems are, however, they shall not detain us. It is more important for us to examine the utilitarian's chief claim—that we ought to maximize the general good or welfare—than to provide a detailed account of the nature of that good. To begin with, let us look at the ethical egoist. He should promote his own individual welfare to the greatest possible extent, being concerned with the welfare of others only insofar as their welfare affects his. Thus, for example, a teacher should want his students to do well only insofar as their good performance does something for him—from the satisfaction of an ego trip to the more tangible reward of a sizable pay raise. But he should not want his students to do well for their own sakes. In short, ethical egoism is the view that people ought to adopt a self-interested attitude toward everything they do.

In contrast, utilitarianism focuses on the general welfare. For example, an egoist supports laws that promote his own welfare to the greatest possible extent. A utilitarian, on the other hand, supports laws for the welfare of everyone. Notice that the utilitarian does not go as far as the altruist who insists that everyone should completely ignore his own welfare in the service of others. Instead, the utilitarian believes that the welfare of all, oneself as well as everyone involved, should be considered. Indeed, each person's welfare should be weighed equally, no one's counting either more or less than anyone else's.

### Welfare and "Illfare"

But this does not mean that every law should promote the welfare of every individual affected by it. Rather utilitarianism requires that the total amount of welfare produced, which is the net balance of welfare over "illfare," should be as large as possible—indeed, in some cases such as controlling an epidemic, the task is to promote the least amount of illfare possible. Thus the principle of utility may well require that some individuals be harmed if the result is of benefit to many others.

Suppose that scientists perfect the procedure for transplanting organs so that it becomes possible to replace just about every organ in the body. The catch is that, in order for a transplant to be successful, the donor must be killed several months before he would die of natural causes. Should we allow such people to be killed? They are dying but they have many healthy organs that could be transplanted. Of course killing them prematurely (assuming they are not experiencing great levels of pain) does not promote their welfare. But the harm done to them is offset by the good that occurs to others. Not only are the recipients of the organs able to live longer but others benefit from their remaining alive—clearly evident when a doctor is able to continue treating people only if he is the recipient of an organ in one of these operations. Although not true in every instance, there would certainly be many where the general good would be better served by killing people and using their organs for transplants than by letting them live out their days. In such cases, the principle of utility requires that the individual be killed so that others may benefit.

We see, then, that the individual plays an ambiguous role in utilitarian theory. On the one hand, he is the basic component, because the general welfare is nothing more than the net total welfare of every individual in the group. On the other, the welfare of some individuals may have to be purchased at the illfare of others. At this critical point, utilitarianism conflicts with the theory of rights. The latter guarantees rights to every individual and does not countenance sacrificing the rights of some so that others can benefit. In this respect, the theory of rights takes the notion of the individual more seriously than does utilitarianism. Moreover, as we see in a moment, the principle of justice also takes the individual more seriously than does the principle of utility.


## *JUSTICE*

The basic idea of justice is desert ( deserving of reward or punishment) or giving everyone his due. Justice is done when people get what they deserve; their desert is based on their acts or the characteristics they possess. Thus a child does not *deserve* punishment because his mother is upset (although children are often punished because of this), but because he treats others wrongly. A person does not *deserve* to go hungry because his country is fighting a war (although people often go hungry because of this and it may be warranted, on grounds other than desert), but because he is unwilling to do his fair share of the work.

But the real focus of the concept of justice, at least as far as social and political thinkers are concerned, is *comparative*—i.e. what one deserves vis-à-vis his peers. Imagine a parent trying to decide what to give her children for Christmas. She would not want to give a train set to one child and a candy bar to another when their deserts are relatively equal. Rather she would want to give relatively equal presents to those who have relatively equal deserts. This idea of *comparative desert* is at the heart of the concept of justice.

We have already seen (ch. 4, § The rule of law) how justice or comparative desert functions in the context of the law. There the idea is to make sure that the law is applied evenhandly—i.e. to make sure that similar penalties are meted out for similar offenses. But here the focus is different; the question is, On what basis should a society distribute its benefits and burdens? In other words, In what way should a society distribute its benefits in order to ensure that everyone is getting what he deserves vis-à-vis the other members of the society?

We note at the outset that questions about the justice of distributions do not arise in all situations. Whenever there is a superabundance, that is, whenever there is more than enough for everyone to have what he wants, there is no problem of distribution. Only when there is not enough to go around, and hence not all people can have everything they want, must attention be given to distribution. Consider air for example. To date, with no shortage of sufficiently clean air, everyone can breathe as much as he needs without affecting others. But if we continue to pollute the atmosphere, we may well reach the point at which there is not enough clean air for everyone. Then we would face the problem of determining how clean air should be distributed. Leave it to a free marketplace which in effect would make the distribution of breathable air a function of one's ability to pay? Give first to the more productive workers? or to those with the greatest need (e.g. people with lung disorders)?

## Justice and Utility

Before examining such questions in detail, however, it is necessary to look at the relationship between justice and utility. As we have seen, utilitarianism is the view that the general good or the general welfare ought to be maximized. Justice, on the other hand, is concerned with how what is produced is distributed. These principles can conflict if it is possible for the maximization of welfare to involve an unjust distribution.

Imagine two different societies. In the first, all goods (wealth, prestige, etc.) are distributed fairly equally. Of course some people have more than others, for it is impossible to eliminate all differences. But the gap between the best off and the worst off is really quite small. In the second society, on the other hand, there are two classes, the haves and the havenots. The havenots do all of the work but have none of the fun while the haves do none of the work but have all of the fun. Yet this society has one redeeming feature: The total amount of benefits is larger than the benefits in the first society. In other words, the amount of welfare enjoyed by the haves so much outweighs the amount of illfare suffered by the havenots, that the net welfare is more than in the society where benefits and burdens are more equitably distributed.

Few people, if any, would deny that the first society is more just than the second. Even though there is considerable disagreement over exactly how much the gap between the haves and the havenots would have to be narrowed in order to achieve justice, there is little or no disagreement that of our two imaginary societies, the one with the more equitable distribution is the more just. And this is so in spite of the fact that the society with the less equitable distribution is the one in which the general welfare is maximized.

*Theory of the Decreasing Marginal Value of Utility*

Most utilitarians feel the need to reply to such examples because they do not want their position saddled with the label of injustice. They point out that in actual practice the kind of situation just sketched cannot arise, because of the theory of the decreasing marginal value of utility. Here's how the theory works. Once the gap between the haves and the havenots exceeds a certain level, it takes more resources to improve the lot of the haves than to improve the lot of the havenots. In other words, the distribution of the available resources to the havenots will produce a greater increase in the general welfare than a similar distribution to the haves.

To see the force of this theory, suppose you have $100 to give away. Would you promote more good by giving it to a millionaire or to someone who is living on the verge of starvation? The answer is obvious. To the millionaire the $100 would not even be a drop in the bucket. But to the man on the verge of starvation, the $100 would make a tremendous difference—for awhile he could eat and feel like a human being; the miseries that attend the approach of starvation would subside and his welfare would take a tremendous change for the better.

The theory is plausible, but there are some problems in using it to insist that the principles of utility and justice cannot conflict with each other. The first is that, as we have seen, the theory only applies when the gap between the welfare of the haves and the havenots exceeds a certain level. Short of that level, it does not apply. Thus, even if one accepts the theory, there will be times when the standard of living for all people is sufficiently similar that $100 will promote as much welfare for the better off as it will for those who are worse off. In such cases, justice may require that all or part of the money be given to those who are worse off; from the point of view of utility, the distribution of the money is a matter of indifference.

At what point does the theory of the decreasing marginal value of utility come into play? This point becomes higher as the number at the lower end of the welfare scale becomes smaller. Thus, if there is a relatively small number of poor people, then spending money on the better-off may well produce more good (given the number of people who will get enjoyment from it) than spending the same amount of money on the poor. For example, to provide luxury housing for the middle class may well produce more welfare than providing decent housing for the poor. And so on.

In addition, the theory of the decreasing marginal value of utility is of no help when the question at issue is, Should welfare be produced immediately or deferred so that more will be available in the future? The utilitarian must forego immediate benefits whenever the sacrifices currently being made will result in a higher level of welfare later. His concern is with the net amount of welfare produced. The advocate of justice, on the other hand, can allow the foregoing of immediate benefits only under more stringent conditions.

To see this, imagine the leaders of an emerging nation faced with the following decision: Should we delay distributing the benefits of industrialization to our people for several generations so that industrial development can proceed at the most rapid pace possible? Or should we distribute the benefits of industrialization as they accrue, thereby ensuring that the rate of industrial growth will be much slower? We can argue for immediate distribution on the basis that the people who do the producing *deserve* the benefits of their production. The plan to delay distribution for several generations cannot be argued for on the basis of justice or desert. Its justification must be on the grounds that the sacrifices made by delaying distribution (i.e. the fact that the current producers are not getting all they deserve), are warranted by the far greater benefits that will be available several generations hence. And this of course is a justification in terms of utility.

### When Justice and Utility Conflict

It is quite clear that the principle of utility often requires the sacrificing of immediate benefits for greater long-range benefits. Why is this incompatible with the principle of justice? As we have seen, justice or desert involves distributing benefits and burdens on the basis of the characteristics that individuals possess. But when one argues that one generation should forego benefits so that there will be more for later generations to distribute, he is *not* justifying the foregoing of benefit on the basis of the characteristics of the individuals involved. His point is simply that it will maximize the total amount of benefits.

The utilitarian is not concerned with the fact that some of the people who make the sacrifices will die before the benefits accrue. All he is concerned about is that the benefits to those in the future will outweigh the sacrifices made by those in the present. Because everyone is to count for one and nobody for more than one, the welfare of every individual involved must be taken into account— but only as part of the "general welfare." The utilitarian has one requirement: The net amount of welfare must be maximized, with each individual's welfare counting neither more nor less than any other individual's. He does not require that the welfare of each individual be maximized.

The principle of justice, on the other hand, is concerned with the welfare of particular persons, not with the total amount of welfare. Justice requires that each individual receive that part of the total available welfare which he deserves (which is commensurate with the characteristics he possesses). Thus, it may be just for an individual to be denied part of the welfare due him today so that at some time in the future there will be more welfare available and *he* will then get a greater net share than he otherwise could. It is not just (although often warranted by utility) to deny part of what is due a person so that at some time in the future *someone else* will get more than otherwise would be possible. As far as justice is concerned, a person getting less than his fair share of what is available at 'one time can only be justified by that *same person* getting his fair share of a greater whole at some other time.

One consequence of this point relates to our economic system. The main argument given in support of capitalism (a free market economy) is that it maximizes the general welfare. Some utilitarians also argue that whatever maximizes the general welfare is just. But I have argued that utility and justice are different kinds of considerations, and that they may well come into conflict with each other. Thus it is possible for capitalism both to maximize the general welfare and to be unjust. It follows that if one is going to argue that a free market economy is just, one must find grounds other than that a free market economy maximizes the general welfare.

### Formal Justice

The concept of justice or comparative desert has been expressed in a variety of different ways. Some speak of giving each his due, some of desert, some of fairness, and some of equality. But common to all these approaches is a basic idea—viz. that justice involves treating equals the same. Thus, if two students do work that is equal in quality they deserve the same grade. If one gets a better grade than the other, the one with the lower grade has every right to complain that he has been treated unjustly. Although most philosophers have concentrated only on this aspect, there is more to the concept. If two students do qualitatively different work, then the grades they get should be different. The one who has done the better work should get a proportionately better grade. Thus justice requires not merely that equals should be treated the same. It also requires that unequals should be treated differently and in direct proportion to the differences between them.

Of course, in any group of people it is always possible to find some respects in which they are the same, even if it is no more than the fact that they are all alive or all human. It is also always possible to find some respects in which they are different, even if it is nothing more than the moment and place of birth. Hence it is not adequate merely to speak of treating equals the same. The concept of equality must be qualified in some way. The grounds for treating people the same must be "equality in certain respects" rather than simply "equality."

But not all respects are relevant to considerations of justice. To use the example of grades once again, if a teacher gives two students the same grade because they have the same color eyes, or the same length hair, or they come from the same city, he is doing something quite perverse. The color of one's eyes, the length of his hair, and the location of his home are not relevant to the grade he should get. For grades, performance on written work, quality of class participation, and perhaps even the amount of effort put forth are relevant. Thus, stated more completely, the principle of justice is: Treat individuals who are equal in the relevant respects the same and treat individuals who are unequal in the relevant respects differently and in direct proportion to the differences between them.

This is simply a formal principle. We say that we should treat individuals who are equal in the relevant respects the same. But this principle can tell us how to act in particular cases only if we supplement it with an account of what respects are relevant. The concept of "relevant respects" functions much the same way that a variable does in a mathematical formula. Until the proponent of justice specifies what respects are relevant, he is not committing himself to much. He is, however, committing himself to something. And because there has been considerable confusion as to what this something is, we dwell on the point for a moment.

Many philosophers have insisted that this formal principle commits one only to acting on general rules.[1] In their view as long as we base our actions on general rules we are being just in a formal way. Thus, as long as we give a ticket to *everyone* who goes over 60 mph., or under 60 mph., or who looks funny when he drives, our ticket giving is formally just. As long as one acts on general rules, no matter what those rules are, he meets the requirement of formal justice.

But the principle of formal justice also requires that these rules be of a certain kind. Consider the following: "Treat everyone who is equal in the relevant respects *and* everyone who is unequal in the relevant respects the same" and "Treat everyone who is equal in the relevant respects *and* everyone who is unequal in the relevant respects differently." Notice that both are perfectly intelligible general rules, yet in addition to being incompatible with each other, they are both incompatible with the formal principle of justice. That principle requires the same treatment for those who are equal and different treatment for those who are unequal whereas the general rules I have just introduced do not. They require the same treatment for those who are unequal and different treatment for those who are equal respectively. There is more, then, to the formal principle of justice than the requirement that one act on general rules (or engage in rule-governed activity). It clearly precludes the following of certain rules. To obtain the principle of formal justice from the requirement that one act on general rules, one must further specify that being unequal can only count as a reason for treating people differently and being equal can only count as a reason for treating people the same.

Even with this specification, however, we have not gotten very far. One of the reasons for developing the formal principle of justice is to isolate the elements that all principles of justice have in common. As we have seen, this isolation is achieved by leaving the variable "relevant respects" completely unspecified. Hence the real problems of justice arise when attempts are made to specify the relevant respects. At this point thinkers radically disagree with each other.

## Material Justice

The variable *relevant respects* in the formula "treat individuals who are equal in the relevant respects the same" has been specified in different ways by different thinkers. These specifications are called material principles of justice. Different specifications, of course, may be appropriate to different situations. Thus the material principle a teacher should use in assigning grades to˙ his students may well be different from the principle that parents should use when distributing benefits to their children. In the case of grades it seems that the kind of work a student does is relevant and hence those who do the best work should get the best grades. In the case of children, on the other hand, it seems that relevance should be specified by either the mere fact of being an offspring, in which case all one's children should be treated the same; or their need, in which case more time, energy, and resources should be devoted to a retarded child than to a child who can get along well on his own. Of course our concern is with the question, On what basis should *a society* distribute benefits, and burdens, among its members? But even within this limited context many different material principles have been proposed; it may well be that different societal benefits should be distributed on the basis of different principles.

### Equality

The call for equality is familiar throughout the history of social and political thought. At first glance it seems to be a cry that every individual be given exactly the same thing. In other words, when faced with the formal principle of justice—treat individuals who are equal in the relevant respects the same and treat individuals who are unequal in the relevant respects differently and in direct proportion to the inequalities between them—equalitarians insist that in the relevant respects there are not inequalities between people. To support this claim they usually point out that although there are all sorts of ways in which people differ from one another, there is one respect in which they are all alike—viz. their humanity (whatever this may mean). Moreover, humanity is the only respect relevant for considerations of justice, and hence it follows that everyone should be treated exactly the same.

Taken literally, this principle is absurd. No one would claim that a person with a ruptured appendix should be *treated in exactly the same way* as a person with inflamed tonsils. Nor would anyone claim that when it comes to military service the infirm should be *treated in exactly the same way* as the healthy. This is not to deny that all people should be treated as human beings. In fact, quite to the contrary, treating persons differently when the situation warrants it seems to be at least part of what is involved in recognizing their humanity. It is important that individuals be treated on the basis of the characteristics they possess, rather than for them all to be treated in exactly the same way.

The equalitarian might well reply at this point that the only reason that his principle sounds absurd is that I have misrepresented it. Of course no one would call for treating people who have different illnesses in exactly the same way. What is important is that they have an equal opportunity to receive medical treatment, not that they receive the same treatment. Understood correctly, therefore, the principle of equality calls for equal opportunity rather than treating people exactly the same.

Equality of opportunity can be achieved in at least two different ways. One is to distribute the wealth equally and leave it up to each individual to decide what he will spend his money on. If this were done, the persons with the ruptured appendix and with the inflamed tonsils could each seek out the kind of help he needs. But what if the treatment for a ruptured appendix costs several times more than the treatment for inflamed tonsils? And what if some individuals make very valuable contributions to society and other individuals make none at all? Should both individuals receive the same incomes?

In other words, it seems that strict equality in the distribution of wealth has the same problems as strict equality in general. There seems to be relevant differences between individuals, and hence proportional equality is preferable to strict equality.[2] But what should serve as the basis of this proportion? Needs, amount of work done, social position? In other words, the principle of proportional equality leaves unanswered the question, What respects are relevant to considerations of justice? and hence is a formal rather than a material principle.

A second and very different approach to equality involves educational and job opportunities. Although agreeing that wealth is the key to opportunity, this approach disdains the idea of regulating incomes—one's income should be a function of the workings of a free market economy. Paramount is making sure everyone has an equal opportunity to get a job. Because education is viewed as the key to vocational success, everyone must also have equal educational opportunities.

But once again there is the problem, Should the equality be strict or proportional? Strict equality requires all children attending schools of the same quality, and hence rules out a system in which black or urban children attend schools inferior to those attended by white or suburban children. But providing all children with schools of the same quality does not help the slow learners, or those who have problems at home which interfere with their schoolwork. Without special help they are bound to end up at the bottom of both the educational and the employment ladder. Similarly, if all children went to schools of the same quality, those with exceptional intellectual capacities could not attend schools especially designed for them.

Do children deserve such a fate? If they were responsible for their slowness, emotional problems, or exceptional intellectual capacities, the answer might be yes. But of course children are no more responsible for these things than they are for being born, and hence it seems that they cannot deserve such a fate.

In other words, equal opportunity in education and vocations must be understood proportionally rather than strictly. There should be different kinds of education for different kinds of children. But what should the basis of this difference or proportion be? I.Q., the ability of parents to pay, the extent of learning disabilities? In other words, What respects are relevant to considerations of justice?

Thus it seems that however the principle of equality is interpreted it is inadequate as a material principle of justice—as a call for strict equality, it is unjust; as a call for proportional equality it is a formal rather than a material principle, and hence raises rather than answers the question, What respects are relevant to considerations of justice?

## Work

The principle of work states that people should be rewarded on the basis of the work they do (i.e. it is work that is relevant to considerations of justice). But what is it about one's work that makes him deserving of recompense? Even if one agrees that work is relevant to justice and hence people who do equal work should receive the same reward, there is much room for disagreement over the respects in which the work must be the same.

One view is that the pleasantness or distastefulness of the work is most important. Some work is quite pleasant and rewarding in and of itself. Consider a skilled surgeon. Day after day he faces new and exciting challenges in his work, and quite often has the feeling of satisfaction that comes from helping people. A fruit picker, ditch digger, or garbage collector, on the other hand, does back breaking, boring and unpleasant work. If those who do the most unpleasant jobs should be rewarded the most, then ditch diggers, fruit pickers, garbage collectors, and the like should be paid more than surgeons, engineers, teachers and so forth.

A second view is that the time and effort one puts into his work are relevant considerations of justice. In this view, the nature of the work done by a surgeon and a garbage collector respectively is not relevant to justice. All that matters is the amount of time spent and the energy expended on the job—for longer and harder hours, more pay; for shorter and easier hours, less pay.

Both these views, and a wide variety of related ones as well, have been advocated by socialist thinkers. Moreover, the arguments against them are usually not in terms of justice. People who reject these views usually argue as follows: Implementation would require either laws that regulate how much is paid for different kinds of work or a totally planned economy. But both of these alternatives have similar drawbacks. To begin with, they are inefficient. Only in a free economy can economic growth, and the increase in the general welfare that accompanies it, be maximized. Second, a planned economy infringes upon individual freedom in a variety of different ways. Every regulation on the marketplace limits some freedom and a publicly owned and regulated marketplace completely eliminates the kinds of freedoms associated with a free enterprise system. In other words, even if such forms of distribution are just, they must be rejected because they do not maximize utility, they restrict important freedoms, or both.

A third view of the principle of work, states that the usefulness of one's work should determine the extent of his reward. In other words, the reward for one's work should be a function of its value to society (as opposed to being a function of the nature of the work itself—e.g. its unpleasantness). Therefore, individuals should receive whatever their peers are willing to pay for their work in a free market economy.

Stated in this form, the principle of work is a species of the principle of utility. Some thinkers are content to leave it at that. Others claim that justice and utility are identical, and hence that whatever maximizes the general welfare is just. I have already argued against this view. Still others accept the distinction between justice and utility and argue that not only does this interpretation of the principle of work maximize welfare, it promotes justice as well. They attempt to show that people *deserve* the rewards meted out by a free market economy in the following way. The reason a free market economy works so well is that it allows those who do the best work to be most successful (This idea is carried to an extreme in the success myth—that anyone, no matter how humble his beginnings, can grow up to be president, a millionaire, or both). Although there is a good bit of luck involved (one must be in the right place at the right time), the underlying idea is that under capitalism those who do the best work will be the most productive and hence (just like cream) will rise to the top in both responsibility and recompense.[3]

But if work is going to serve as the criterion of just distributions, it would seem that the reward for one's work should be a function of both his ability and his effort. After all, suppose someone became very successful in business, not because he worked hard or because he had any ability or talent, but simply out of sheer luck. Perhaps he married the boss's daughter. Or perhaps he is the only redhead working for the firm and the boss has a redhead fetish. Or perhaps he makes some very unwise decisions which, as a result of completely fortuitous and unforeseeable circumstances, turn out very well. It would seem that in these circumstances an individual does not deserve to rise above his peers either in authority or in income. In the distribution of society's basic benefits and burdens, what a person *deserves* should be a function of what he does and is responsible for, not a function of fortuitous happenings.

There are two main problems with the capitalist's interpretation of the principle of work as basis for distribution. First, although this principle may be acceptable in a situation where everyone who wants to work can, it seems unacceptable when work is not available to all who desire it. If it is in the nature of our economic system that 4 to 5 percent of the work force must be unemployed (whether they want to be or not), it seems unjust to allow the unlucky ones, who cannot get work, to starve. Possibly a subconscious awareness of this point has led to the belief, at least in the United States, that everyone who is out of work is lazy and shiftless. If this were true, then it would be at least plausible to claim that those who are out of work deserve their fate—they are unemployed because they are lazy. But if it is not true, as current social theory seems to realize, then it is hard to see how justice is served when those who do not work cannot have an income at all.

There is, however, a second far more serious problem with the capitalist's interpretation of the principle of work. Its implementation inevitably produces conditions which make the principle unacceptable. I have argued that, for the principle to be acceptable, one's work must be a function of his ability and effort, not of luck. But one of the consequences of basing distribution upon work is that inequalities develop between the wealth of various families. Moreover, wealth clearly gives a person an edge when it comes to competition in the economic sphere. The person who begins a business venture with a lot of capital behind him has far better chances of success than someone with very little money. This is obviously true for a lot of reasons, not the least of which is that the more capital one has, the larger is the margin of error within which he can operate. Thus the person with wealthy parents has a much better chance of making a lot of money himself than does someone whose parents are poor. But of course you have no control over whom your parents are. It is simply a matter of chance that you are born to rich parents rather than poor ones (or vice versa).

One might well reply that, although this line of argument is correct, there is a very simple way to get around the problem. Prevent (perhaps through very stiff inheritance taxes) parents from passing their wealth on to their children. In this way, although individuals could reap the benefits of their own work (which we are assuming they justly deserve) they could not pass these benefits on to their children, and hence they could not give their children an advantage which they cannot be said to deserve.

Unfortunately, the solution is not so simple, First, to enact this kind of inheritance tax would destroy much of the motivation to work that makes the capitalist's conception of the principle of work so attractive. If parents cannot provide their children with advantages that they never had, then there is no need for them to work nearly so hard. Second, it is an oversimplification to think of the advantages which parents give their children (and which as we have seen, the children cannot be said to deserve) simply in monetary terms. Intelligence, motivation, initiative, etc., play a role in how successful one becomes and are primarily a function of one's parents (either because of heredity, the environment they provide at home, or both). Hence it is not really possible to provide all people a fair chance when it comes to work. How well they work is to a large extent a function of chance factors over which they have no control; therefore, how they make out economically cannot be a function of what they deserve.

*Need*

According to this principle, distribution is just when it is based upon need. In other words, people should be treated the same when their need is the same, and they should be treated differently in direct proportion to the inequalities between their needs. This is not to say that everyone must have their needs equally met; in most cases it is impossible for society to meet the needs of individuals—only the individuals themselves can. In other words, although society can provide all people with the opportunity to eat a well-balanced diet, it cannot force them to do so. Although society can provide all people with educational opportunities, it cannot force anyone to become educated (although it can force them to go to school). And so on. Thus the principle of need requires that all individuals be given the opportunity to satisfy their needs to the same degree. Whether or not they utilize this opportunity is a different matter entirely.

This principle is often referred to as the communist principle of distribution. Although Marx discusses the concept of need, it is at least doubtful that he viewed it as a principle of distribution.[4] But there can be no doubt that Lenin as well as many of Marx's other followers viewed the principle of need in this way. As Lenin says:

The state will be able to wither away completely when society has realized the rule: "From each according to his ability; to each according to his needs," *i.e.* when people have become accustomed to observe the fundamental rules of social life, and their labour is so productive, that they voluntarily work *according to their ability*. "The narrow horizon of bourgeois rights," which compels one to calculate, with the hard-heartedness of a Shylock, whether he has not worked half an hour more than another, whether he is not getting less pay than another—this narrow horizon will then be left behind. There will then be no need for an exact calculation by society of the quantity of products to be distributed to each of its members; each will take freely "according to his needs."[5]

In order to fully understand and assess the principle of need, one should begin by asking the question, What are needs? For an answer to be adequate it should analyze the related concepts of "wants" and "desires" as well as that of "needs."[6] I simply offer the following definition: To say "I need $X$" is to say "without $X$ I am lacking in some way that is detrimental to me." I hope that, in the discussion that follows, you will get an idea of the significance and content of this definition.

To begin with, the advocates of the principle of need assert the necessity of providing the opportunity to meet what can be called "essential needs"—such as for food, clothing, shelter, uncontaminated air, and whatever else is necessary for survival. But the advocates of the principle of need do not stop here. Sustaining people in life without making any attempt to make that life good is simply not enough. Keeping someone alive so that he may lead a life of squalor and suffering is very cruel. In other words, if justice requires that people have the opportunity to meet their essential needs, it also seems to require that they have the opportunity to make their lives worth living.

Of course the question immediately arises: How far must society go in this direction? Usually the answer is that society must also provide people with the opportunity to meet their "basic needs." In other words, of the needs that exist above and beyond essential needs some are basic and some are not; and justice requires that the basic needs be provided for.

It becomes imperative, then, that we be able to distinguish between basic and nonbasic needs. Yet this task is extremely difficult at best, because it pre-supposes that some needs are more important than others, and hence that some things are *really* needed while others are not.[7] But once you get beyond needs that are necessary for survival, there just does not seem to be any clear-cut way of distinguishing between what is really needed and what is not. After all, a family of eight can survive in a two-room shack. Do they need a ten-room house, a television set, a car, a family vacation? There does not seem to be a fully adequate criterion for answering these questions.

**Created Needs:** Another approach distinguishes between essential and created needs (rather than between essential and basic needs). What are created needs? Those which are created within individuals either by the physical development of their society or by the standards of goodness their society develops. Consider, for example, a car. Because industrial societies have developed physically so that most residential areas are set off from industrial areas, a means of transportation is a necessity for almost everyone desiring a job. Given the dreadful state of mass transportation in many of these areas, a car is often the only means of transportation that will do. For those people who could not get to work without a car, or who cannot get a job because they do not have a car, we can speak of a car (or at least an adequate means of transportation) as a created need. This need for survival (i.e. an essential need) does not result directly from the demands of the human body. Rather it is created by the way in which the society has developed. Hence we can call it a "created essential need."

On the other hand, there are created needs of a far more subtle nature, which reflect the standard of the good life that develops within a society. Primarily through the influence of mass communication there are a whole host of things that people feel they need in order to make their lives satisfying and complete—a house (perhaps two), a television set, a two-week vacation, and so on. When people cannot have these things they feel that they have been hurt in a significant way. In short, as the standard of living rises, people feel the need to live at a higher level of affluence. To those who can afford it, there's not much of a problem. But to those who cannot, the problem looms large. It's not merely that they cannot have what they feel they need; rather, they are constantly reminded of their inability by the affluence around them. Perhaps it is better to be poor in an underdeveloped country than in an affluent one. At least in an underdeveloped country one's hard physical existence is not supplemented by the mental torment caused by living in the midst of luxury.

Of course created needs must be distinguished from mere wants and desires. One way would be to limit the concept of created needs to those things necessary for survival (i.e. created essential needs). But this would be no more adequate than limiting the concept of need to essentials which has already been rejected. Hence it is necessary to find a way to distinguish between nonessential created needs and mere wants and desires. But now we're back to the same problem that plagues the attempt to distinguish between basic and nonbasic needs. Once you get past the concept of essential created needs, there just does not seem to be any fully adequate way of determining where created needs leave off and mere wants or desires take over.

In addition to the problem of developing an adequate concept of need, there is a more practical problem involved in advocating the principle of need as the material basis of justice. Some people who believe that the principle of need is just also believe that it is impractical. They believe that if people know that their needs will be provided for regardless of whether they work or not, then they will not do any work. In other words, people need to be prodded to work—they will only be productive if the incentive of profit is dangled in front of them.

As we have seen (ch. 4, § Human Nature: Unchangeable? Does It Exist?), this position can be attacked either by arguing that human nature is not as these people perceive it, or else by arguing that there is no set and unalterable human nature. If people will work without the incentive of profit, then of course there is no problem. If, on the other hand, there is no set and unalterable human nature, then people are motivated by profit only because of the society in which they live. If that society is changed and the people are educated (or conditioned) in the appropriate way, they will be able to function perfectly well without the incentive of profit.

### Need and Work: A Compromise

As indicated above, many people think that the principle of need is the most adequate material principle of justice even though they also feel it is impractical—it fails to provide an incentive to work. Some of these people turn to a compromise between these two principles often referred to as the welfare state. They attempt to combine the principles of need and work in a way that they feel retains the best elements of each. The basic idea of the welfare state is that although a competitive market system is best, it is unjust to simply ignore the lot of those who lose out in the competition. A way must be found to provide a minimum standard of living for even those who cannot work. Be it in the form of a welfare system, an income maintenance assistance plan, or a negative income tax, the basic idea is the same. The unemployed should not be allowed to languish in poverty or starve to death. Justice requires that a way be found for them to survive at a minimum standard of decency.

The justification for this view relies on the principles of both work and need. Work, in the capitalist's sense of the principle, should be the basic principle of distribution. Yet at the same time society has an obligation to provide for at least the essential needs of all its members. Hence distribution should be based upon need up to the minimum standard to which everyone is entitled. From that point on, work should be the sole determinant of distribution. Such a procedure takes cognizance of the view that need is relevant to considerations of justice. Yet at the same time it also takes cognizance of the belief that without the incentive of profit, people will not work. This latter point is the reason why all such plans are assessed in terms of whether or not they destroy the incentive to work. If one can make more by not working than by getting a job, then something is wrong. The system must be so arranged that it is to the advantage of everyone who can get a job to do so. For it is only in this way that the principles of work and need can function in concert with each other rather than at cross purposes.

However, this approach does not eliminate the basic problem that plagues the concept of need. In order for the welfare state to represent a genuine compromise between the principles of need and work, there must be a level at which the principle of work replaces the principle of need as the basis for distribution. If this level is set too low (if, for example, the principle of work replaces the principle of need once everyone is provided with the opportunity to meet their essential needs), the proponents of the principle of need will object. As shown above, they will claim that about all the compromise principle does is to preclude allowing people to starve to death. They will argue that there is something very cruel about keeping people alive so that they can languish in poverty; hence, if people are going to be kept alive, there is an obligation to provide them with the opportunity to make their lives reasonably enjoyable.

If, on the other hand, the level is set too high (if, for example, the principle of work replaces the principle of need only after everyone is provided with the opportunity to meet *all* needs) then the proponents of the principle of work will object. They will claim that although society may have the obligation to provide individuals with the opportunity to meet some of their more basic needs, there is no obligation to provide the opportunity to meet all needs. They will insist that setting the point at which the principle of work replaces the principle of need too high is unacceptable because it does not leave enough room for individual achievement and initiative.

Thus it seems that for the compromise between the principles of work and need to be both acceptable and genuine, the principle of need must refer to more than the essential but not to all needs. But this raises once again the basic problem that we have seen plaguing the principle of need. Exactly which needs, above and beyond essential needs, should all people be given the opportunity to satisfy? And indeed, this is a main focus in the debate over the welfare state. If a minimum standard of living is going to be guaranteed to all people, at exactly what level should that minimum standard be?

### A New Approach: John Rawls

In his challenging and exciting book, *A Theory of Justice*, John Rawls presents a different answer to the question, How should the benefits of society be distributed?[8] His proposal, which is in the equalitarian tradition, is that all inequalitites in the distribution of benefits must be justified; and that such inequalities are justified only if they work to the advantage of those who come out on the short end of them (i.e. they should work to the advantage of the least advantaged members of society). As a result, Rawls sees the justification for inequalities in a radically different way from the utilitarian and the advocate of the principle of work. Consider the distribution of money. According to the utilitarian, that some people have more money than others is justified if the condition produces the greatest possible amount of welfare. To the advocate of the principle of work, that some people have more money than others is justified if people are rewarded on the basis of the work they do. To Rawls, however, that some people have more money than others is justified only if the standard of living of those at the bottom of the economic scale is raised to a higher level than it would be without the inequality. Thus, for example, a free market economy produces a just distribution only if competition increases productivity to such an extent that wages (especially of those at the bottom of the economic scale) are increased at a faster rate than would be possible under any other kind of economic system.

I have already argued that benefits should be based upon characteristics that people are responsible for, and not upon mere matters of chance. This is the reason why, if it is to be a plausible candidate as a material principle of justice, the principle of work must be tied to ability and effort. This is also the reason why, if individuals are denied work simply because there are not enough jobs for everyone and they just happened to be in the wrong places at the wrong time, then it is not fair to say "no work, no income."

Rawls seizes upon this point and carries it even further. He points out that tying work to one's ability and effort does not really result in basing distribution on characteristics for which individuals are responsible. A person's ability and the kind of effort he is willing to make are largely the result of what Rawls calls "the natural lottery."[9] An individual has no say about the talents he is born with—these are simply a product of heredity. Moreover the abilities an individual develops as he matures are to a considerable extent a product of the environment in which he is raised. So too is the amount of effort he puts into his job.

Some children grow up in an environment which helps instill in them a burning desire to succeed, while others grow up without really being motivated to do anything.

In other words, hereditary and environmental factors play a very large role in determining the kind of worker an individual is. They influence the abilities he has and the amount of effort he puts into his job. But these factors are the result of chance or the natural lottery. It is entirely a matter of luck that an individual is born to a given set of parents and raised by them. Hence one does not deserve the characteristics which come from hereditary and environmental factors. And since ability and effort are to a considerable extent the product of such factors, they cannot be the characteristics upon which a just distribution is based.

It follows that the same considerations, which lead to the modification of the principle of work in terms of effort and ability, when carried to their logical conclusion, lead to the total rejection of the principle of work. Of course, at this point Rawls could turn to the principle of need. But he avoids the kinds of problems attendant on the principle of need by turning in a very different direction.

He argues that if it is true that people should not be rewarded on the basis of their ability and effort because they cannot truly be said to be responsible for them, then we should view ability and effort (as well as the work that results from them) in a very different light—as community resources. As such, they should be rewarded not on the basis of what the individual can command with them, but rather on the basis of the good they can do for the community. If it is to the advantage of the community to pay more for a given talent, then this should be done. But to say that something is to the advantage of the community is to say that it is to the advantage of everyone. And because Rawls assumes that whatever benefits the least advantaged members of society also benefits everyone above them (but not vice versa), inequalities are justified in his view only if they work to the advantage of the least advantaged members of society.[10]

This summary is at best too brief; Rawls takes over six hundred pages to develop his position. But I hope I have presented enough of the position to indicate how Rawls's theory differs from the other theories of justice I have presented. With these different theories as background, you should begin the process of determining for yourself what the material content of the principle of justice should be.

*NOTES*

1. For example see Chaim Perelman, *The Idea of Justice and the Problem of Argument*, trans. John Petrie (London: Routledge & Kegan Paul, 1963), chs. 1-3.

2. For a discussion of proportional equality see Aristotle, *Nicomachean Ethics*, trans. Martin Ostwald (Indianapolis: Bobbs-Merrill, 1962), book V.

3. Do the best workers actually get to the top under capitalism? Consider, for example, the Peter Principle: In a bureaucracy every employee tends to rise to his level of incompetence (as opposed to competence). For a development and discussion of this principle see Laurence F. Peter and Raymond Hull, *The Peter Principle* (New York: William Morrow, 1969).

4. For a discussion of this point see Robert Tucker, *Philosophy and Myth in Karl Marx* (Cambridge: at the University Press, 1961).

5. V. I. Lenin, *State and Revolution* (New York: International Publishers, 1932), pp. 79-80.

6. For an interesting attempt, see David Braybrooke, "Let Needs Diminish that Preferences May Prosper," *Studies in Moral Philosophy*, American Philosophical Quarterly Monograph Series (Oxford: Basil Blackwell, 1968), pp. 86-107.

7. For an interesting attempt to do this, see Herbert Marcuse, *One-Dimensional Man* (Boston: Beacon Press, 1964), ch. 1.

8. John Rawls, *A Theory of Justice* (Cambridge, Massachusetts: Harvard University Press, 1971).

9. Ibid., pp. 73-74.

10. Ibid., pp. 79-83.

# 6

## Limitations on Sovereignty and Government

So far our discussion has focused upon the various advantages which are said to accrue from living under the authority of a sovereign who affects his sovereignty through a government. These advantages—the procurement of effective freedom, the guaranteeing of natural rights, the maximization of the general welfare, and the achievement of a just distribution of benefits and burdens—have been offered by philosophers as the justification for living under the authority of others. As we have seen, however, there are problems with each of these purported justifications. On the conceptual level, we must figure out exactly what freedom, rights, welfare, and justice involve. On the normative level, we have to determine which of these notions is the ultimate end or, if more than one of them is ultimate, how to resolve conflicts among them. And on the practical level, we need to determine the best way to transcribe these ends into institutions and laws.

In addition, another kind of problem has yet to be considered. In the state of nature everyone is pretty much on an even footing with his peers. An individual finds that, while some people prevail over him, he prevails over others. The point is that the state of nature is competitive, and the competition is fairly even. At least no one is *given* an edge over anyone else (although some undoubtedly have an edge through their natural endowments).

But with the establishment of a sovereign (be it a dictator or the people) all of this changes. An authority is established who has the right to impose his will on everyone. And a government is set up to allow the sovereign to effect his will. Although man's lot is improved, there is also a risk that it could become worse rather than better. If the sovereign is evil, or unintentionally makes bad decisions, everyone is in trouble. In the state of nature, evil people or bad decisions have limited effects—they only affect those who are closely connected with them. But in civil society, by having an authority over the people, we ensure the fact that everyone is affected by his decisions. That is all well and good if he makes good decisions. But what if he doesn't?

Of course this problem does not arise under individual sovereignty (anarchism). Under such a system sovereignty remains in the hands of individuals. But the problem does arise under both dictatorial and popular sovereignty. As a matter of fact, however, most proponents of dictatorial sovereignty are not concerned with limiting the authority of their sovereign. For example, both Plato and Hobbes believe that the authority of the sovereign should be unlimited.

In popular sovereignty, on the other hand, the situation is quite different; all proponents begin with individual sovereignty, and recognize the importance of individual rights. If the people's sovereignty is unlimited in scope, given that the will of the people is the will of the majority, then the door is wide open for the majority to tyrannize the minority (or individuals). All proponents of popular sovereignty want to prevent tyranny of the majority from arising, and hence they all propose limiting the sovereign's authority in some way.

## THE NONINTERVENTION PRINCIPLE

There are many varieties of the nonintervention principle. Common to all of them is the idea that the scope of the sovereign's authority should not be absolute—that is, there are certain areas in which the sovereign should not have the right to interfere in the lives of the members of society. The proponents of this view generally believe that the area of nonintervention should be as wide as possible. However there is considerable disagreement among these thinkers about the questions, How much can the scope of sovereignty be limited without destroying the benefits that accrue from living under a sovereign authority? and What is the justification for imposing limits on the sovereign's authority?

### Arguments for Limiting Authority:
### Natural Law, Happiness, Freedom

The claim that limitations should be placed on the sovereign's authority has been argued in three main ways. The first is in terms of the theory of natural rights or natural law (see ch. 4, § The Theory of Natural Rights). One function of natural law theory is to set down basic rights for all individuals, and, as we have seen, an argument given for living under the authority of others is that only in this way can your natural rights be protected against violation by peers. Here, however, we are concerned with these rights vis-à-vis the duly constituted authority. *In this context, the theory of natural rights establishes a set of fundamental individual rights that not even the sovereign can violate.* In dictatorial sovereignty, this means that there are some things (such as taking life or property) that the dictator has no right to do to his subjects. In popular sovereignty, it means that there are some things that the people have no right to do to members of the society.

One of the procedures for protecting natural rights against the sovereign is to turn them into legal rights by writing them into a constitution. The best possible protection is provided by a set of rights written into a constitution that cannot be amended. But it should not be inferred that, if a constitution can be amended, it offers no protection whatsoever to the rights embodied in it. There are all sorts of ways to make it difficult to amend a constitution without making it impossible. And of course the more difficult the amending process is, the better protected are the rights set down in it. Consider, for example, a system of popular sovereignty in which a simple majority is required on all votes save those that involve amending the constitution. For such votes a majority of two-thirds, three-fourths, or even more could be required. The higher one sets the required margin for amendments, the better is the protection given to the rights embodied in the constitution.

The second main argument for the nonintervention principle is in terms of happiness or the general welfare. As formulated by John Stuart Mill, the argument is that each individual is in the best position to know what will make him happy.[1] If the sovereign is given the chore of determining what will make people happy, more often than not he will be wrong. And if by chance he should be right, it is very unlikely that he will be able to bring about happiness through his actions. This is true no matter how small the government machinery may be. But the larger the bureaucratic machinery, the less is the chance that a sovereign will make his people happy by having the government do things to or for them. Mill concludes that the way to maximize each individual's happiness is to leave him alone as much as possible. And since the general happiness is no more than the net total of individual happiness, this will maximize the general happiness as well.

The third main argument for the nonintervention principle is in terms of individual autonomy or freedom. The basic idea here is that although it is desirable to sacrifice as much individual autonomy as is necessary to reap the advantages of living in society, it is also desirable that as little individual autonomy as possible be sacrificed. Such autonomy is held to be an end itself, as are the advantages gained in society; hence only as much autonomy as is absolutely necessary should be sacrificed. This is just another way of saying that the sovereign's power should be no more than the minimum required to reap the benefits of social life, that the area of nonintervention should be as large as possible. Now it is time to look at the different forms the nonintervention principle takes.

Although it is not possible to examine every species of the nonintervention principle, it is possible to look at the three main criteria—harm to others, harm to oneself, offensiveness—for limiting the scope of the sovereign's authority. These criteria provide an idea of both the variety of forms the nonintervention principle takes and the problems involved in trying to spell out exactly what the scope of the sovereign's authority should be.

## Harm Principle

The basic idea of this principle is that the sovereign's authority only extends to those actions which involve harm to others (see ch. 3, § Negative Freedom). He should interfere with such actions. But he should not interfere with actions that do not involve harm or, if they do, only involve harm to the agent himself. In this view, the sovereign is pretty much relegated to the role of peacekeeper. He should stop me from assaulting or killing someone else. But if I choose to mistreat myself, the sovereign should not interfere. If he does not like what I am doing, or even if he thinks it immoral, he should not interfere. Only when my actions involve harm to others should he step in and force me to behave in a certain way.

Although this is easy enough to say, the actual application of the principle is not easy. Although there are some acts that clearly do not involve harm to others (e.g. cleaning one's fingernails), and some acts that clearly do involve such harm (e.g. murder), there are numerous cases in which it is not at all clear whether or not harm is being done to others. Does being mean to someone constitute harming them? What about smoking in another's presence, setting off firecrackers, exposing oneself in public, working in a gun or napalm factory? The main task facing the proponents of the harm principle is to delineate the dimensions of harm so that these questions, and numerous others like them, can be answered.

Even without such delineation, however, we know that there are many ways in which societies deviate from the harm principle. According to the harm principle, there should be no laws that prohibit homosexual practices between consenting adults, although there perhaps should be laws against homosexual seduction and clearly against homosexual assault. There should be no laws that require the wearing of safety helmets while riding a motorcycle, although there should be a law that prohibits selling a defective helmet to an unsuspecting customer. There should be no laws that proscribe attempted suicide, although there should be laws that proscribe attempts on the lives of others.

## Preventing Harm to the Whole Society

According to the harm principle, the sovereign should also interfere to prevent harm to society as a whole (public harm). Not only does he have the responsibility of protecting individuals against the attacks of their peers, he also protects his sovereignty and the institutions through which it is effected against the attacks of those who would like to destroy them. This responsibility not only gives the sovereign the right to protect the state against those who seek to destroy it through acts of treason and sabotage, it also gives him the right to raise the money necessary for running the government machinery.

There are some obvious cases of what constitutes public harm—for example, sabotaging the country's transportation system, fouling its water supply. But there are many others in which it is not clear whether a public harm is being done. Does criticizing your country's war effort constitute public harm? What about refusing to pay the share of your taxes that goes to support space exploration? Or refusing to deed over your land to the government so that a new superhighway can be built? And so on. Proponents of the harm principle must address themselves to these public dimensions of the principle.

### *Using Harm Principle to Justify Questionable Practices*

In recent times, at least in the United States, the public harm principle, in the name of either domestic or international security, has been used in an attempt to justify highly questionable practices. Jailing thousands of demonstrators even though the authorities know in advance that they will bring charges only against a mere handful; carrying on an undeclared war and keeping actions secret primarily because, if the actions are made public, authorities anticipate an outpouring of criticism at home; spying on presidential candidates and seeking to undermine their candidacies by a host of "dirty tricks"—these and other such acts have been carried out in the name of the public harm principle, that is, in the name of either domestic or international security.

These practices are not merely unfortunate; they are dangerous. Because such acts seem to bend the public harm principle all out of shape, they lead some people to reject that principle altogether. But the principle is not at fault; rather, the fault lies in the way it is being applied by those in power. There are legitimate concerns of security, and it would be a real disaster if people ignored them out of the fear that, to acknowledge them, opens the door to misapplication by the government.

Not only must proponents of the harm principle distinguish between private harm (i.e. to individuals) and public harm (i.e. to society), they must also distinguish between direct and indirect harm. Some acts, for example assault, directly cause harm to others while others, for example driving while intoxicated, merely create a risk that harm will occur. One can argue either that the sovereign has the right only to prevent those acts that cause direct harm or that he also has the right to prevent those acts which create a sufficiently high risk (however this may be determined) that harm will occur (indirect harm).

Applying these principles leads to quite interesting results. The advocate of the direct harm principle must believe that, even if drug addiction causes acts which involve harm to others, the sovereign has the right only to proscribe those acts; he does not have the right to proscribe the sale or use of drugs (the only direct harm the sale or use of drugs involves, if it involves any, is to the user himself). He also must believe that even if there is a high correlation between the possession of handguns and harm to others, the mere possession of a handgun should not be outlawed.

The proponent of the indirect harm principle, on the other hand, can maintain that if the use of drugs and possession of handguns is closely correlated with harm to others, then both the possession and the sale of these things can be proscribed. Notice that I have said that the proponent of the indirect harm principle *can* maintain this position, not that he must. Whether or not he does should depend upon how close a correlation exists between drugs and handguns on the one hand and harm to others on the other (i.e. how great a risk is run by not proscribing their sale and possession), and how great a risk of harm he believes must exist before the sovereign is justified in taking action (i.e. at what point on the scale of risks he believes the principle of indirect harm becomes operative).

Thus although the direct harm principle places fairly narrow limits on the scope of the sovereign's authority, the indirect harm principle considerably broadens this scope (i.e. it lessens the defined area of nonintervention). Another and even more significant way of broadening the sovereign's authority is to supplement the harm principle with some other principles. We discuss two, paternalism and offensiveness.


## Paternalism

The view that the sovereign has the right to act to prevent the individual from harming himself is called paternalism. The basic idea is that the sovereign is like a parent who knows what is best for his children. He leaves them alone as long as they are not doing anything that will result in harm to themselves. But when he sees that they are going astray he exerts his authority. After all, no parent likes to see his children suffer.

At universities, a familiar form of paternalism exists when the institution functions *in loco parentis* (in the place of the parent). Many universities feel that it is their responsibility to intervene just as a parent would when students are doing things that will result in harm to themselves. Thus they attempt to prevent pot smoking, sexual expression, cutting classes, etc. The assumption is that these things will harm the students themselves and that the university, like a parent, has the responsibility to protect the student from himself.

It is often pointed out that our society is paternalistic in a variety of ways. Consider the familiar example of laws which require motorcycle riders to wear safety helmets. Clearly they cannot be justified in terms of the harm principle. Their sole justification is that they are for the good of those who wear them. If these people will not do it of their own accord, they should be forced to. Or consider the proscription against marijuana. If marijuana is outlawed in the belief that pot smoking leads to drug addiction, and drug addiction leads to crime, then its prohibition can perhaps be justified by the indirect form of the harm principle. If, on the other hand, it is prohibited in the belief that it will harm the user, then although its prohibition can be justified by paternalism, it cannot be justified by the harm principle.

Behind paternalism is the idea that the individual does not really know what is best for himself. The clearest case is when someone acts out of ignorance. Suppose I am traveling along a mountain road and that, unbeknownst to me, there is some blasting going on in the vicinity which creates a hazard of landslides. Should I merely be warned of the dangers ahead, or should I be prohibited from traveling the road even when I decide I want to travel it in spite of the dangers? It seems that although I should be warned of the full extent of the dangers that await me, I should not be prohibited from traveling the road if I so choose. After all, some people find life more exciting when risk is involved. If that turns me on, then why shouldn't I be allowed to do my own thing? Of course if the state wants to prevent travelers from taking the road in order to save the expense of having to mount a rescue mission in the event that something should happen, they can simply inform me that no rescue mission will be mounted. If I still want to go on should be my decision.

Once I know about the dangers ahead I no longer act out of ignorance, but perhaps there is another problem. After all, who in his right mind would want to travel a road after being informed that there is a good chance of landslides? If there is something wrong with my mind (whether I am insane or just acting irrationally), perhaps the state would be justified in interfering to prevent me from harming myself.[2]

Let us consider someone who wants to commit suicide—he is not sick or even overly depressed; he just does not feel like living any more. Of course if anything constitutes harm to oneself it is suicide, and hence the paternalist believes that the sovereign should interfere in such cases. In order to justify such intervention, the paternalist often insists that it is impossible for a sane person to attempt suicide. In other words, everyone who attempts suicide is irrational, and therefore it is legitimate for the sovereign to interfere with such actions.

This line of argument is circular; it provides no independent test of sanity. Irrationality is defined simply in terms of the desire to commit suicide. This definition makes it logically necessary that all people who desire to commit suicide are irrational; this is unacceptable. It may be that, as a matter of fact, everyone who desires to commit suicide is irrational, but this is different from defining the one in terms of the other. In the former case, we first decide what constitutes rationality and then examine all the people who desire to commit suicide to determine whether or not they meet this criterion. It may be that none of them do. But this finding would not be because we have defined irrationality in terms of the desire to commit suicide; rather it would be because we have observed that only irrational people attempt suicide. There certainly is no logical reason why a perfectly rational person could not desire to commit suicide even if, as a matter of fact, most of the people who attempt suicide are not rational.

So far I have argued both that there are many paternalistic laws in every society and that it is not legitimate for the advocate of paternalism to justify such laws by insisting that anyone who would want to act contrary to them must be insane or irrational. But the paternalist can still fall back on the more general claim that the average person simply is not rational,[3] and hence paternalistic laws are justified. This same argument, of course, is used against both individual and popular sovereignty. In that context, it is claimed that people are not capable of governing themselves. But in that context, it at least makes sense because, given the conflicts that can arise between individuals, it may be that people are incapable of governing themselves. However, it is hard to make sense out of the sweeping claim that people are incapable of acting rationally even in matters that concern only themselves.

### Offensiveness

Some thinkers maintain that the state can interfere with the offensive actions of its citizens. This argument is usually given for banning books, closing down pornography stores, prohibiting prostitution, and the like. The mere fact that members of a society find these things offensive is sufficient reason for prohibiting them.

It is important to distinguish carefully between offensiveness and harm as principles for taking action. It sometimes is maintained that homosexual practices should be outlawed not merely because they are offensive, but because they lead to harm. If homosexual practices caused sexual attacks, then they could be outlawed on the grounds that they lead to harm to others. Or if homosexual practices turned our young adults into a group of sissies who would not fight to defend their country against foreign invaders, then they could perhaps be outlawed on the basis of public harm. But if homosexual practices have none of these undesirable consequences, and there is no evidence that they do, then some other ground must be found for outlawing them. The fact that people find them offensive is the one most often offered.

It is also important to distinguish between the offensiveness of public and of private acts. It is one thing to be offended by the *sight* of someone exposing himself in a public place and quite another to be offended by the *thought* of someone "exposing" himself in the privacy of his home. If offensiveness is accepted as a reason for prohibiting certain acts, it is far more difficult to argue that the state should prohibit those acts which are offensive *and which take place in private* than it is to argue that the state should prohibit those acts which are offensive *and which take place in public*. To eradicate offensive practices from private places—to make sure that pornography is not read, marijuana not smoked, and offensive sexual practices not engaged in, even in private places— would be very costly indeed. And even if not costly, it would require the kind of total surveillance system described so graphically by George Orwell in *1984.*

A second, equally important dimension of public offensiveness must also be considered. It is one thing to have pornography books mixed in with others in our bookstores, so one might come across them unexpectedly and be offended. It is quite another to have clearly marked pornography stores, or clearly marked sections in bookstores devoted to pornography. There is something quite per- verse about the person who looks through book after book in store after store to find one that he can claim offends him. There does not seem to be any reason why those who seek out things to be offended by, just so they can complain that they are offended, should be protected from themselves.

This case is clear, but as usual there are a whole host that are less so. Suppose there is a very high-class house of prostitution in town—well kept, no solicitation on the streets, no bums loitering around the house, and so on. In short, there are none of the attendant evils that usually go with such enterprises. Nevertheless everyone knows what kind of a house it is. Can someone claim that the mere fact that there is such a house, or that it is in his neighborhood, or that he must pass it on his way to work, offends him? Is this sense of "offensive" enough to make it legitimate to close down the house?

Before you answer too hastily, consider the following: If being offensive in this sense is sufficient for closing down the house, then it would seem that husbands and wives should be prohibited from doing things that are offensive even in the privacy of their own bedrooms. Nevertheless there is a difference between the person who actively seeks things that he can say offend him and the person who is offended by what goes on next door, or around the corner. Even though we do not want to say that if the mere thought of something offends people it should be prohibited, we may well want to say that people should be protected from the sight and sounds of things that offend them.

Thus far, we have seen how offensiveness, paternalism, and harm can be used to limit a sovereign's authority. Now we turn to the problem of controlling the government's power.

## LIMITATIONS ON GOVERNMENT

Both dictatorial and popular sovereignty require a government through which the will of the sovereign can be effected. But the establishment of a government with the power to carry out the will of the sovereign creates the possibility that the government may ignore that will and impose its own will upon the people. Thus, under both dictatorial and popular sovereignty there is a need for safe- guards against the usurpation or appropriation of the sovereign's power by the government.

Although this problem arises under both dictatorial and popular sovereignty, the risk of usurpation is far greater under popular than under dictatorial sovereignty. Under the latter, the sovereign is the head of the government; he has trusted officials who report directly to him; the only way in which his power can be usurped is if these officials turn on him. Under popular sovereignty, on the other hand, the sovereign and the government are distinct entities. The people elect individuals to run the government, and it is run by these individuals rather than the sovereign (i.e. the people). Although the need to have safeguards against the usurpation of the sovereign's power has not been totally ignored by proponents of dictatorial sovereignty, it is of far greater concern to proponents of popular sovereignty. It is a central and dominant theme in all such theories.

But there is a more important difference between the roles that usurpation plays in dictatorial and in popular sovereignty. Under dictatorial sovereignty, if the sovereign's power is appropriated by another government official, all that happens is that one dictator replaces another. The form of the state remains unchanged. When the people's power is usurped by the government (or, more correctly, government officials), however, the form changes from popular to dictatorial rule. Because our concern at this point is with protecting the rights of the people and of individuals against the government, it is only the usurpation of power under popular sovereignty that need concern us.

It may seem that one way of providing protection against usurpation is to write the appropriate limitations on the function of government into a constitution. But simply setting down limitations on governmental authority in a constitution does not by itself provide any real guarantee that the government will adhere to such limitations. Because the real power (i.e. the police and military) is in the hands of the government, the people would be practically powerless if the government decided to overstep the limits set down by a constitution. What is really needed is a governmental structure which precludes, or at least renders highly unlikely, that kind of usurpation.

## *Separation of Powers*

By investing different powers in different branches of government, and by allowing these different branches to serve as checks on each other, the government can be restrained from overstepping its (constitutional) limits and ignoring the sovereignty of the people. Typically, the powers of government are separated into the three main functions—legislative, executive, and judicial. The legislative function, as the name implies, is to enact laws, the executive to enforce laws and keep peace, the judicial to interpret the law and punish its violators. When all these powers are in the hands of a single-branched government, that government is very powerful. It can pass whatever laws it chooses, use the police and military to enforce the law in any way, and then support both the enactment and the mode of enforcement of these laws through its judiciary function. It would not be at all difficult for such a government to ignore the sovereignty of the people.

But when these different functions are invested in different branches of the government, and each of the branches, although having its own basic function, also serves as a check on the other branches, it is far more difficult for the government to usurp the power of the people. Some thinkers have proposed that, although passing legislation should be the main responsibility of the legislative branch of government, all legislation should have to be approved by the executive and subjected to the scrutiny of the judiciary with respect to its constitutionality. That although the adjudication of conflicts should be the main responsibility of the judicial branch, both the executive and the legislature should have a voice in determining who the judges will be. And that although law enforcement should be the main responsibility of the executive branch, what laws are enforced and the appropriation of the funds for financing law enforcement should be the responsibility of the legislature. Under such an arrangement, it is far more difficult for the government to usurp the power of the people.

This protection, however, is purchased at a price. Although a government based upon the separation of powers is less of a threat to the people, it is also less efficient. If the executive could implement programs without having to depend upon the legislative branch to appropriate funds to support them, he could implement them more rapidly and carry them out more consistently. Or if the legislature could pass laws that do not require the signature of the executive, legislation could be approved far more rapidly. Of course, the decisions made by a government in which there is a consolidation of powers are not necessarily better than the decisions made by a government in which there is a separation of powers. But the need for cooperation among different branches of government does render it more difficult to achieve goals. The more branches involved, the more interests must be accommodated. And the more interests that must be accommodated, the more compromises that have to be made and the longer it takes to reach a decision.

Some people take these difficulties attendant to the need for compromise as a reason for strengthening either the executive or legislative branch of government. But the more one strengthens a given branch or the more one consolidates the functions into a single branch, the greater is the chance that the power of the people will be usurped by the government. The basic problem of popular sovereignty is to strike a balance between the efficient operations of government and the protection of the sovereignty of the people. The main vehicle for protecting the sovereignty of the people is the separation of powers, but it is important that powers not be separated so drastically that the government cannot carry out its job of effecting the will of the people in both domestic and international affairs.

When President Nixon authorized the fighting of an undeclared and secret war in Cambodia, he was violating the doctrine of the separation of powers as I have described it.[4] Not only is the legislature, rather than the executive, charged with the responsibility of declaring war, but it is also the legislature's responsibility to appropriate funds. The legislature was appropriating funds for a military venture in Vietnam, but they were not appropriating funds for a war in Cambodia. Yet the President ordered that some of the appropriated funds be used in Cambodia. Of course the president's view was that the war in Cambodia was necessary for the success of the Vietnam venture. He felt it was his responsibility as commander in chief to help U.S. forces in Vietnam in whatever way was necessary. Yet he also must have felt that it would be difficult to get the legislature to appropriate funds for a war in Cambodia. Thus the president sought to circumvent the check that the legislature imposes on his war-making power by issuing secret orders. Whether or not the United States should have been fighting in Cambodia (or Vietnam for that matter), it is important to realize how directly the president's decision to pursue that war secretively undercut the separation of powers. And because it undercuts this separation, it necessarily raises concern about the extent to which the people's sovereignty is being usurped by the government.

## Pluralism

The proponents of popular sovereignty are also concerned about protecting individuals against the power of the people. In other words, they want to guarantee that there will be an area in which the sovereign (i.e. the people) cannot interfere in the lives of individual members of the society. One way of doing this is by including a set of individual rights in a constitution (e.g. the U.S. Bill of Rights). As long as the constitution can be amended, however, there is the chance that through the amending process the majority will violate the boundaries set down by the nonintervention principle.

Another way of coming to grips with this problem is to employ the idea of pluralism. In one sense, the mark of a pluralistic society is that a great variety of viewpoints are held by different individuals. A number of social and geographical characteristics contribute to pluralism in this sense—everything that tends to unite people works against it whereas everything that tends to create differences between people reinforces it. Thus, a country in which all people share a common ethnic background is less pluralistic than a country where the people have many ethnic backgrounds. A country where most people do the same type of work is less pluralistic than a country with a highly diversified economy. A small country with a uniform climate and geography is less pluralistic than a larger country with diversified climate and geography.

But there is a second and stronger sense of "pluralism" in which it functions as a check against the oppression of individuals; in this society, avenues are kept open so that those individuals or groups with differing views have an input into governing the country. If minorities cannot influence decisions, then they can easily be tyrannized by the majority. But if minorities can influence government decisions, then their interests will be at least partially accommodated by the government.

### Coalitions

The most effective way to provide minorities with this kind of input is to structure the system in such a way that no overall majority view emerges. Of course there are majority views; otherwise majority rule would be impossible. But although there is a majority view on each particular issue, the individuals who constitute that majority are different from issue to issue. In other words, the majority is composed of shifting coalitions among minorities rather than of an unchanging group of individuals who impose their will upon everyone else.

The need for coalitions, which is the basis for this kind of pluralism, greatly increases the power of minority groups. These coalitions can function at both the legislative and the electoral levels. At the legislative level coalitions are required whenever there is no majority view in the legislative body; they must be formed either to establish governments or to pass legislation. Of course the more views there are, and the more evenly these views are represented in the legislative body, the more influence minority groups can have in drafting and enacting legislation. On the electoral level, coalitions must be formed among different groups to develop support for candidates. To be elected, a candidate must broaden his base of support (some call this "appealing to the lowest common denominator"), and make commitments to support the needs and demands of different groups. To be successful nationally, a party must put up local candidates who reflect the interests of the people of their region, and put up national candidates who reflect a wide enough variety of interests to get them elected. This is why people with many different viewpoints—hawks and doves, integrationists and segregationists, etc.—are found within the same political party.[5]

### Limiting Constituencies

The most prominent way to allow for representing different views in the governmental process is to limit the constituencies which elect government officials. If every candidate for office is elected by the same constituency, and if there is a majority view in that constituency, then it is highly likely that everyone elected will hold the majority view. But if candidates are elected by different constituencies, then only if the majority view nationally is also the majority view *in every constituency* (which is highly unlikely) will all the elected candidates hold the majority view.

The United States is an example of a country in which pluralism is effected by regional representation. The president is elected nationally, senators on a statewide basis, and congressmen by districts within states. As a result each has a different constituency. This arrangement not only helps to provide checks and balances, it also promotes pluralism. The election of senators is designed to ensure that the interests of the states will be represented in the Senate, the election of congressmen that the more limited interests of regions within states will be represented in the House of Representatives.

It is easier, then, for minority groups to gain seats in the House of Representatives than in the Senate. Also, a minority group thinly spread throughout the nation has more trouble getting input into the governmental process than does a minority group concentrated within a particular district. This fact is the main pitfall in effecting pluralism through regional representation. But it nevertheless is true that a government based on regional representation provides far greater protection to minority rights than one in which all officials are elected by the same constituency.

It follows from all of this that in a pluralistic system the primary function of legislators is *not* to act upon what is best for the country; it is to further the interests of the groups that elected them. Legislators are indebted to the voters—and soon learn that Legislation is the art of compromise. Each legislator and each group gives in here to get concessions there. For this reason, as the proponents of Black Power clearly recognize, blacks must not expect to make political gains within the United States because their cause is right. The way for them to make gains is by capturing and skillfully using political power. Only by organizing the black community behind black candidates, by refusing to support white candidates who do not care about black liberation, and so on, will blacks attain a position of strength in the bargaining for votes, which is the essence of pluralism.

The main threat to pluralism is obviously the development of parties or groups so strong that they do not have to make concessions to get their way. This threat can come from either of two sources. On the one hand, in spite of the pluralizing effect of regional representation, a majority view may in fact arise. Indeed the more integrated a country becomes—the more the well-being of each region depends upon the well-being of other regions and of the nation as a whole—the more likely it is that this threat to pluralism will arise. On the other hand, a group—for example, the so-called military-industrial complex—may, by the use of such tactics as propagandizing the public, lobbying, and buying votes with campaign contributions, in effect impose its view on either the people or the legislature. A system only remains pluralistic to the extent that it can prevent these kinds of abuses.

Unfortunately, however, the security for minorities gained from a pluralistic system is not without its price. Whenever legislation must result from compromises between competing interest groups, that legislation will tend to be enacted slowly and conservative in nature. The only time that one can expect fast, forceful action is in emergencies that are national in scope; in these cases the interests of all groups tend to coincide. But with regard to needs of a more limited nature—for example, power shortages in a restricted area, agricultural problems, urban blight, and so on—the situation is very different. They are of real concern only to limited groups; hence, in order to get action on them, the group involved usually has to settle for less than the optimum and must support the interests of other groups on other issues. For this reason, under pluralism, solutions are seldom as good as they could be, and sometimes are delayed almost to the point of uselessness.

### The Dissonance of Power

The problems raised by both the separation of powers and the idea of pluralism can perhaps best be understood in terms of the tension that surrounds the role of government within a system of popular sovereignty. Government is most efficient when power is concentrated in the hands of a ruler or a ruling group. Without the separation of powers and the need to cater to the interests of particular groups, the ruler can act both swiftly and uncompromisingly to achieve his goals. Moreover, he can act on his perception of what is in the interest of the country as a whole, rather than in terms of pounding out a compromise among different interest groups. Of course this concentration of power allows for and greatly increases the possibility of usurping the sovereign power of the people and of oppressing minority groups.

Thus the fundamental challenge for proponents of popular sovereignty is to find ways of protecting both the sovereignty of the people and the rights of minorities while at the same time not preventing the efficient operations of the government. It is clearly an open question whether or not the separation of powers and pluralism is the best way of treading the thin line between inefficient government on the one hand, and ignoring the sovereignty of the people and the rights of individuals on the other. But there can be no doubt that this is what they are intended to do, and hence they should be assessed in terms of how well they do this job.

### NOTES

1. John Stuart Mill, *On Liberty* (Indianapolis: Bobbs-Merrill, 1956), ch. 4.

2. The positive conception of freedom (see ch. 3) allows that when I am not in my right mind, the state can interfere with my actions because to do so makes me free. In the positive view it is relatively easy to justify paternalism. But in the view of freedom developed here, where the absence of external constraint is the crucial condition, the justification of paternalism is far more difficult.

3. Recall our discussion of Plato, ch. 2, § Rule by Truth of Philosopher King.

4. This is not to say that the doctrine of the separation of powers as laid down in the U. S. Constitution was violated, although it may have been. We are not concerned with the legal issue. The point is simply that this action violated *the concept of the separation of powers as I have described it.*

5. This is also why the candidacies of Barry Goldwater (1964) and George McGovern (1972) for president of the United States were such dismal failures. Both Goldwater and McGovern refused to broaden their base of support by "watering down" some of the views they held. As a result they appealed to a very limited constituency, and suffered overwhelming defeats.

# 7

## Marxism (Communism), Fascism, and Democracy

In this chapter we examine the basic tenets of marxism (communism), fascism, and democracy with three main goals in mind: first, to lay bare the theoretical underpinnings of these theories; second, to make clear how the basic concepts of social and political thought discussed in preceding chapters function in these different theories; and third, to help eliminate many of the misconceptions which surround these theories. In the process, the basic challenges facing each theory are brought to light.

### MARXISM (COMMUNISM)

To begin with, it is imperative to distinguish communism from marxism. The term *communism* is used in two different ways of concern to us. On the one hand it refers to the operating sociopolitical systems in the so-called communist countries—Russia, China, Cuba, East Germany, etc. On the other, it refers to the variety of sociopolitical theories presented by the so-called communist thinkers—Marx, Lenin, Mao, Castro, etc. From what has gone before, you know that the concern of this book is with the justification of different kinds of sociopolitical systems rather than with the examination of the way such systems function in different countries. Thus the focus will be upon the theory of communism and its justification rather than upon existing communist societies and the way they operate.

Even within the framework of this kind of concern, however, there are two different approaches that can be taken. One can either try to develop the core set of principles common to all communist theories or else focus on the theory of a particular communist thinker. Partly because there may be no significant core to all communist theories, and partly because looking for such a core would leave untouched much that is interesting in the theory of the most influential communist thinker of all, Karl Marx, I shall take the latter approach. I shall simply attempt to analyze the theory of marxism. Thus I shall make no claims concerning the extent to which particular communist societies adhere to or deviate from Marx's ideas—although this is something to which you should give considerable thought. Nor shall I make any claims concerning the extent to which followers of Marx (Lenin, Stalin, etc.) have remained faithful to or deviated from his principles. I shall simply attempt to present some of Marx's basic ideas, recognizing that any brief summary must necessarily leave many important things unsaid.

Like all thinkers, Marx's ideas developed over time. Marx's early writings, the so-called *Economic and Philosophic Manuscripts* (1844), did not come to light until well after his death, and have only come under the close scrutiny of scholars since the 1950s. Because there is a difference in both emphasis and temperament between these and his later writings (the former seem to reflect the sensitivity of a humanistically oriented philosopher, the latter the impersonal calculation of a social scientist), much controversy has arisen over the relationship between the early and the later Marx.[1] As interesting as this controversy is, however, the issues are too complicated and obscure to be pursued here.

### Social Materialism

Whatever changes as Marx's thought develops, at least one element remains constant, his materialism. "Materialism" here does not refer to *psychological materialism*, the view that all human acts are motivated by the desire for material things (i.e. wealth and the things it can purchase); nor does it refer to *crass materialism*, the view that only material things are worthwhile; nor to *metaphysical materialism*, the view that everything that exists is material and hence there are no spiritual entities such as the soul, God, etc. Rather it refers to Marx's *social materialism*, the idea that the way to understand the thoughts and actions of people is not to examine those thoughts and actions in their own right, but rather to examine the conditions which produced them.

Marx is quite explicit on this point.

We do not set out from what men say, imagine, conceive nor from men as narrated, thought of, imagined, conceived, in order to arrive at men in the flesh. We set out from real, active men, and on the basis of their real life-process we demonstrate the development of the ideological reflexes and echoes of this life process. The phantoms formed in the human brain are also, necessarily, sublimates of their material life-process, which is empirically verifiable and bound to material premises. Morality, religion, metaphysics, all the rest of ideology and their corresponding forms of consciousness, thus no longer retain the semblance of independence.[2]

In other words, Marx believes that the real significance of concepts and thoughts lies, not in the ideas themselves, but in the conditions that produced them. Thus, the significance of the "right to life" lies in the conditions that have led people to believe there is such a right, rather than in any kind of natural law. The key to understanding the concept of God lies in the conditions that have led people to believe in an all-powerful being, rather than in theological percepts and teachings. Or more generally, Marx believes that the way to understand history is *not* to look at the great ideas of influential statesmen, but rather to examine the conditions that produced those ideas. Thus, for example, the way to understand the freeing of American slaves by President Lincoln is *not* to look at the humanitarian ideas expressed in the words of the Emancipation Proclamation, but rather to look at the conditions (i.e. the economic conflict between the north and south) which produced both the institution of slavery and its abolition.

Marxism may sound like typical social science fare: man is a product of his environment; hence if you want to understand man's actions and beliefs you must study his environment, and if you want to change those actions and beliefs you must change that environment. But it is a mistake to think of Marx's view in these terms. The conditions Marx speaks of are what he calls "material conditions," and these constitute only one component of what we normally think of as "environmental conditions."

The way in which men produce their means of subsistence depends first of all upon the nature of the actual means they find in existence and have to reproduce. This mode of production must not be considered simply as being the reproduction of the physical existence of the individuals. Rather it is a definite form of activity life, a definite form of expressing their life, a definite *mode of life* on their part. As individuals express their life, so they are. What they are, therefore, coincides with their production, both with *what* they produce and *how* they produce. The nature of individuals thus depends on the material conditions determining their production.[3]

In other words, the most important thing about an individual is the work he does, and the most important thing about a society is the work its members do. One's life is his work, and society's life is the work of its members. This work is a function of two main factors: (1) the physical environment—for example, individuals in an area with rich soil tend to be farmers whereas those near well-stocked lakes and streams tend to be fishermen; and (2) the kind of economic system—free market, planned, etc.—within which people work. When working conditions differ in these two regards, then the work is different in character; the beliefs of individuals and the nature of their society is a function of the character of this work.

### Alienation

In his early writings, Marx developed this interesting, important concept.[4] It is his view that alienation is a product of capitalism and the only way to eliminate it is to destroy capitalism. Moreover there are three basic ways of being alienated: from the product of one's labor (he also calls this alienation from nature), from the productive activity of labor (alienation from oneself), and finally from the species (from others). We examine each of these aspects in turn.

## Alienation From Product of Own Labor (Nature)

When a person is alienated from the product of his own labor, the product develops an independent existence; it stands opposed to him as an autonomous power, dictating to him rather than being dictated to by him. In order to understand what it means for the product of labor to have an independent existence, imagine a farmer and his family who lead a completely self-sufficient existence. Everything they grow or make, they use for themselves; everything they consume is of their own making or production. They grow their food, make their clothing, and build the structures they live in. Every bit of work they do is for their own survival and comfort; they use all of the products of their work for these purposes.

Compare with this a society in which people survive by consuming products that others make, and produce things for others to consume. This situation exists whenever production is in terms of the division of labor. Each person produces one kind of thing, or in more sophisticated systems one part of one kind of thing, and in return earns the means of subsistence. Although such a system is compatible with a barter economy (i.e. where there is no money and people trade goods and services), it is certainly facilitated by the introduction of money. For then everyone works for money, and can use it to purchase what they want.

Whenever one produces simply for his own consumption, whatever he does not consume will not be used at all. Under this system the use of products is completely tied to the person who produces them. When products are made for others, however, consumption is completely independent of the person who produced them. They are bought and sold by others for the use of others. Hence they come to exist in their own right, totally independent of the person who produced them.

Marx claims that these products also come to stand opposed to the workers who produce them as an autonomous power; dictating to the workers rather than being dictated to by them. It is one thing to produce those items for yourself which are necessitated by the circumstances of your life; it is quite another to work so that you can consume whatever items are available in the market place. In the former case, you produce the essentials of life for your own consumption. In the latter, you work to possess what are often luxuries dangled in front of you by others.

In other words, Marx believes that capitalism enslaves people to the products of production by continually creating needs in them for those products.[5] The moment one makes enough to get something that he has wanted for a long time, there are ten other things on the market that he wants even more. In short, rather than producing goods that they need, the people are conditioned to need those goods that are produced. Thus what is produced dictates what people need or want when, really, needs or wants should dictate production. The poor strive to satisfy created needs while ignoring some of their basic needs. Thus, good nutrition is ignored in the pursuit of flashy clothes or an overpowered car. On the other hand the rich often work themselves to death pursuing the wealth necessary to meet their created needs. The moment a person is able to purchase a home in suburbia, the pressure mounts to join a country club, travel to Europe, build a second home, and so on. People are never content because their needs or desires increase faster than their ability to satisfy them.

If Marx thought of the product of one's labor only in terms of being an autonomous power opposed to him, then alienation from this product would simply be a function of created needs. And he might reason as follows: If needs cannot be created, then alienation from the product of one's labor could not exist. Even if needs can be created, alienation could be eliminated simply by halting this process. But Marx also analyzes alienation from the product of one's labor in terms of the mere independent existence of products. Because of this, he believes that alienation can only be eliminated when individuals (or at least families) live on a self-sufficient basis (i.e. although labor may be divided within a family, it is not divided within society as a whole). Marx says that man should live in harmony with nature, each individual making use of nature to meet his own needs. This is why he also speaks of alienation from the product of one's labor as alienation from nature.

### Alienation From Productive Activity of Labor (Oneself)

This second aspect of the concept of alienation makes the individual unhappy with his work; he finds it boring and monotonous rather than interesting and challenging. In contemporary industrial societies, this alienation is evidenced by high absenteeism, poor performance on the job, high rates of alcoholism and drug use among workers, and so on. Because the worker is alienated from the productive activity of labor and experiences inner turmoil, Marx also refers to this aspect as alienation from oneself. Just as alienation from the product of one's labor puts one at odds with nature, so alienation from one's productive activity puts him at odds with himself.

As Marx sees it, there are two main causes for becoming alienated from oneself. First, people no longer work for themselves. Under capitalism most people work for others. As an employee, work is not exciting or fulfilling; an employee invariably feels that he is doing all the work while his employer gets all the benefits. In a small retail establishment, for example, the owner almost always takes a much greater interest in, and gives much better service to, the customers than do his employees. For the owner, the business is his life; for the employee, his job is simply a means to life.

Second, Marx claims that alienation from oneself is also caused by the division of labor. The more limited the scope of the tasks one does, the less exciting and challenging the job is. Which would you rather do, build entire cars or simply put the doors on cars? Because the building of a car requires the performance of a great variety of tasks, the work is diversified and challenging. But if you are only putting doors on, the work quickly settles down to a boring routine. Of course the division of labor increases efficiency (at least up to a point), but it also produces the boredom and restlessness that are the manifestation of alienation from oneself.

### Alienation From the Species (Others)

According to Marx, man is a *species-being*. He means that all individuals must be viewed as part of a group; man in isolation is a completely meaningless abstraction. In effect Marx is taking a middle ground between the organic and atomistic conceptions of the state (see ch. 2, § The State and the Individual). He is claiming that mankind should not be viewed as a group of totally independent individuals or atoms. At the same time, however, a group of individuals should not be viewed as an organic unity in which the group is more than the sum total of the parts that make it up. Rather, says Marx, each individual should be viewed in the context of the community in which he lives, because the nature of each person can only be understood in terms of the ways in which that individual interacts with others and with the institutions around him. Mankind's basic goal is survival as a species or a community, and it is through the cooperative interaction of all individuals within that community that this goal is best achieved.

Marx insists that under capitalism each man is turned against other men and against the species. Each individual is in a constant struggle with his peers to possess the fruits of labor necessary for survival. As a result there is neither community activity nor concerted effort to ensure the survival of the species. If the species does survive, it is luck. As people become isolated from each other, the population explosion, the environmental crisis, the arms race, etc. develop and threaten to continue unchecked. Only when individuals view themselves as part of a species and seek to preserve that species can we have the kind of cooperative activity that precludes alienation from the species.

### Alienation: An Assessment

Marx believes that alienation is the product of capitalism and that, if we eliminate capitalism, alienation will cease. But it is not at all clear that he is right. Suppose we eliminated the division of labor and developed an economy in which people did whole jobs rather than bits and pieces of them. Suppose further we broke society down into small units and each unit only produced the essentials of life for its own consumption. We would still be faced with the struggle for survival. Indeed, given the inefficiencies in such a mode of production, the struggle for survival would probably be heightened. Marx seems to be suggesting that this form would be the ideal (unalienated). But would it really be an improvement?

In other words, as we have seen, Marx seems to think that the real fly in the ointment is the division of labor. Remember that he lived during the early throes of the industrial revolution. At that time it was not unusual for people to work fifteen to eighteen hours a day and merely make enough to keep alive. Since then, times have changed; the benefits of the division of labor have begun to accrue to the worker. He can now buy more and live better than he could without the division of labor. Of course this may be a mixed blessing. Not enjoying one's job while living within the spiral of constantly increasing needs may not be the best possible life. But the question remains, Is doing away with the division of labor an improvement or a step backward? If the latter, maybe we can humanize the work process while retaining the division of labor. If this is not possible, man is condemned to choose between high productivity and unrewarding work on the one hand and low productivity but more rewarding work on the other.[6]

A second problem with Marx's account of alienation arises from his view that the most fundamental thing about an individual is the work he does. It follows that if an individual is alienated in his work then he is an alienated individual. In contrast to Marx, one could argue that alienated work, although undesirable in itself, does not necessarily result in an alienated individual. Of course it will if a person has to work fifteen to eighteen hours a day six or seven days a week. But with a forty-hour work week (and this figure is declining), the situation is quite different. Work is much less important because less time is devoted to it. Under such conditions it is possible to argue that, although work may have to be alienating, the individual is not necessarily alienated. By engaging in meaningful and stimulating pursuits in his leisure time the individual can lead an unalientated existence even though he is alienated in his work.

### The Dialectic

In his later writings, Marx goes in a different direction. Instead of attempting to answer the questions just raised, he turns his attention to economics. He attempts to develop a theory that will show that capitalism inevitably leads to communism. However, underlying Marxist economics and the critique of capitalism it entails, is a more fundamental theory that ties the movement of history to economics. Marx develops his social materialism into a fullblown theory of economic determinism;[7] he developes a general theory of history which gives real substance to his social materialism. He does this by adapting the idea of the dialectic as presented by Hegel[8] to his own purposes. For Hegel the dialectic is the reasoning process; it pertains to our ideas and how they develop. For Marx, given his materialism, this is nonsense. If we want to understand the development of ideas we must look to the material conditions in which those ideas are spawned rather than to the ideas themselves. Hence the dialectic must be applied to material conditions. Because he changes the locus of the dialectical process in this way, Marx claims to have stood German idealism on its head.

As described by Hegel, the dialectic is a three-stage process. It involves a thesis, an antithesis, and a synthesis. The thesis (the first stage) generates an antithesis which, as the name suggests, comes into conflict with the thesis. The result is a third stage (the synthesis) which is the result of the working out of the conflict between the thesis and the antithesis. As applied by Hegel the thesis is a thought which generates a thought which conflicts with it, and the result or synthesis is a new idea which resolves this conflict. For Marx the thesis is a given socioeconomic arrangement, the antithesis is an economic class that develops and comes into conflict with that system, and the synthesis is a new arrangement which results from the conflict between the old system and the antagonistic class. This process moves on inexorably; each system necessarily sowing the seeds of its own destruction (i.e. generating a conflicting class) and being replaced by a new system.

Although Marx gives many illustrations of· this process, the only one that need concern us is the transition from capitalism to communism. Marx claims that just as capitalism grew out of feudal society with the bourgeoisie (the craftsmen who populated the growing cities) serving as the catalyst (or antithesis), so communism will grow out of capitalism with the proletariat (the working class) serving as the catalyst. This is because under capitalism the worker is a wage-slave of the capitalist. The worker has no money at all and must work for whatever the capitalist will pay him (barely enough to remain alive). Hence the worker is completely powerless. If he quits his job he will starve to death; if he makes any trouble, either by asking for more money or attempting to unite with other workers, he will be fired and will starve to death. In short, the worker is entirely at the mercy of the capitalist.

Moreover Marx believes that, as capitalism matures, the gap between the capitalist and the worker will continue to grow. The capitalist will get richer and richer while the worker continues to live at a mere subsistence level. And as capital becomes consolidated into fewer and fewer hands, there will be fewer and fewer capitalists and more and more proletarians. Eventually there will be only a handful of capitalists and a mass of proletarians. At this point the workers will revolt. It will be a violent revolution because the capitalists will not give up their power willingly. The institutions of capitalism will be totally destroyed and a classless society will emerge. Because there are no more classes, there will be no more conflicts to fuel the dialectical process. Hence communist society will not be subject to the destructive forces that have brought down all previous societies.

Obviously, things have not turned out under capitalism as Marx predicted. For whatever reasons, the worker has not become a totally depraved being entirely at the mercy of the capitalist. But remember that Marx was writing (*Communist Manifesto*, 1848) long before the inception of the labor movement and the rise of the middle class. At that time it may well have been reasonable to think that the worker could never become anything more than a pawn of the capitalist.

This of course in no way alters the fact that Marx was wrong. Perhaps he was wrong because he began with an inadequate view of history—that economic classes provide movement dialectically. In other words, it may be that to fully understand history one has to take into account more than simply economic factors. Or it may be that history is not deterministic as Marx claims, and hence historical prediction is no more than a guessing game. Or it may be that, although his theory of history is correct, he did not fully understand the factors at work within that theory and thus failed to see the direction in which events were inevitably moving.

But whatever the reason, Marx was wrong; hence, if marxism is to be an acceptable theory, it must be revised. The most promising direction for this revision to take is to deemphasize (or even reject) the theory of history which has been viewed as the core of marxism and to emphasize the theory of alienation developed early by Marx. It seems fair to say that all three aspects of alienation cited by Marx—from the product, from the productive activity, and from the species—exist in modern industrial society. Thus it would seem that the most effective way to make marxism relevant to modern society is to try to show that alienation is a product of, or at least contributed to by, capitalism. If it can be shown that a classless society would reduce alienation, then capitalism should be rejected. If, on the other hand (as our discussion of alienation seems to suggest), alienation is primarily a function of the kind of work required in an advanced industrial society, then to replace capitalism with a classless society will not reduce alienation. If this analysis is correct, people should alter the kind of work required by modern industrial society rather than alter the economic system.

### Communist Society

When it comes to describing communist society, Marx is not very helpful; his main concern is to show that capitalist society is in the process of destroying itself. When this destruction occurs, it will be replaced with a classless society.

What will this classless society be like? How will power be distributed? What form of sovereignty will prevail? What kind of rights will be guaranteed? And so on. Marx does not really address himself to these issues. In spite of this failure, or perhaps because of it, Marx's followers have dealt with these issues in considerable detail. But the result has been a very mixed bag. Some embrace anarchism, others popular sovereignty. Still others speak of the need for a dictatorship over the proletariat until such time as the people become capable of ruling themselves, yet they give no indication of when this will happen.

Because Marx's concern is to show how history inexorably moves toward the day when the capitalists will be overthrown by the workers, he does not spend any time at all discussing the concept of authority or legitimate power. For Marx the important question is not, Who has the right to rule? but rather, Who is and will be in the position to rule? Under capitalism, no matter how things may look in theory, the capitalists have the power; those with the money run the show politically as well as economically. Even where capitalism is coupled with representative government, the right to vote merely gives the worker the chance to choose which capitalists will oppress him. When the revolution comes, however, the capitalists' power will be destroyed and the workers will gain control. Marx believes this is necessarily going to happen, and hence the question of its justification simply does not arise.

## FASCISM

Although it seemed wise to limit our discussion of communism to a specific species of that doctrine (viz. marxism), this approach is not germane to our discussion of fascism. *Fascism* is used in the generic sense of the term; the discussion focuses on the basic tenets common to all theories of fascism rather than on a specific species of the doctrine. Of course this approach results in overlooking the differences between different species of fascism. Thus, for example, the fact that German fascism (nazism) was racist while Italian fascism was not will be ignored. But it seems to me that what is common to all species of fascism is more important than what distinguishes them; and it is on these commonalities that I focus.

Fascism begins with an organic theory of the state and, by utilizing the positive conception of freedom, develops a theory of dictatorial sovereignty. As you recall, the organic theory of the state is the view that the state is like an organism in the sense that the whole is more than the sum total of its parts (i.e. the individuals who make it up). Each of the parts gets its meaning or signifi-cance by virtue of its relationship with the whole, but the whole is not reducible to the parts that make it up. As Mussolini says:

In Fascism man is an individual who is the nation and the country. He is this by a moral law which embraces and binds together individuals and generations in an established tradition and mission, a moral law which suppresses the instinct to lead a life confined to a brief cycle of pleasure in order, instead, to replace it within the orbit of duty in a superior conception of life, free from the limits of time and space a life in which the individual by self-abnegation and by the sacrifice of his particular interests, even by death, realizes the entirely spiritual existence in which his value as a man consists.[9]

Human life, viewed independently, is transient and meaningless. But by identifying oneself with the entire history of a people, by binding oneself together with other individuals and generations in a tradition and mission, one gives real meaning and permanence to his existence. According to the fascist, this identification, with a group that has a common mission and tradition, cannot be explained in material terms. Thus, one cannot understand this common tradition in terms of the material conditions that produced it (as Marx claims); further, this common tradition and mission are more than the lives and desires of the individuals who make up the group. There is some kind of spiritual entity, usually referred to as either the national spirit or the general will, which exists above and beyond the individuals who make up the nation. This national spirit, because it is not reducible to the individuals who make up the nation, must be understood in its own right and on its own terms. Moreover it is this spirit that gives meaning to the lives of individuals. Because the individual is a part of this entity, which transcends his limited time on earth, his life has real meaning and significance.

### The Roles of the Leader and the Individual

But how is it possible to determine what the national spirit or the general will is, what the mission of a nation is, and whether or not particular acts or policies fit in with that mission? According to Rousseau, the way to discover this spirit (he calls it the general will) is to take a vote.[10] But Rousseau is not a fascist. The fascist view is that the task of discovering and pursuing the national spirit is the job of one man (or a small group of men). This point is very instructive. It shows us that, although there is no necessary connection between the organic theory of the state and the rule of one man, as a matter of fact the two are conjoined in fascist theory.

Thus the fascist believes that every state or society has a specific mission to pursue. The pursuit of this mission, as discovered or interpreted by the leader, is most important. Individuals may be sacrificed in the pursuit of this mission; they are expendable. But in being done away with, individuals are in fact achieving real significance. They are playing their part in the development of the national spirit.

For Fascism, society is the end, individuals the means, and its whole life consists in using individuals as instruments for its social ends. The state therefore guards and protects the welfare and development of individuals not for their exclusive interest, but because of the identity of the needs of individuals with those of society as a whole. We can thus accept and explain institutions and practices, which like the death penalty, are condemned by Liberalism in the name of the preeminence of individualism.[11]

To say that the individual exists for the state is ambiguous. If one analyzes the state in terms of popular sovereignty, it means that ultimate authority rests in the hands of the people and it is up to the people to determine and implement the national spirit. As we have seen, however, fascists analyze the state in terms of dictatorial sovereignty. The national spirit is discovered or interpreted by the leader, and he may take whatever steps are necessary to see that that spirit is realized. Hence the ruler decides which forms of individual sacrifice are necessary for the good of the nation. Moreover, the individual should not resist the ruler; by following the leader's instructions (even if they involve sacrificing his life), the individual becomes identified with the national spirit and his existence is given more than fleeting significance.

To serve the nation by doing whatever the ruler deems necessary also liberates the individual. Because he adopts the positive conception of freedom (see ch. 3, § Positive Freedom) the fascist insists that to be free is to act in accordance with the higher self. Moreover the higher self is identified with the national spirit or general will. Because the individual is not capable of determining the national spirit, nor would he always follow it if he did perceive it, the individual only is liberated by the person who is capable of discerning the national spirit and who forces him to follow it. In other words, it is the fascist view that a person acts freely when he follows the dictates of the ruler.

Note how well the organic theory of the state and the concept of positive freedom lend themselves to the abuses characteristic of both the theory and practice of fascism. When the organic nature of the state manifests itself in the guise of a grandiose mission and purpose for the people, as it usually does, fascism is a doctrine of expansionism, aggression, and domination. And when the mission of the state requires many sacrifices of and by individuals, as it usually does, fascism embraces the violation of individual rights, so often associated with positive freedom.

## Fascism and Marxism

Before concluding it is helpful to contrast fascism with marxism. Marxism is basically an economic theory of history which attempts to show that capitalism will eventually be replaced by a classless society. Fascism, on the other hand, is basically a sociopolitical theory about the nature of sovereignty and the state. This is not to deny that the marxist may embrace dictatorial sovereignty (as does the fascist) nor that the fascist may reject capitalism in favor of a classless society (as does the marxist). But marxism is also compatible with the idea of popular sovereignty, and fascism with capitalism. Furthermore, there is more to marxism and fascism respectively than the ideas of a classless society and dictatorial sovereignty. To advocate dictatorial sovereignty is quite different from advocating fascism. You are only a fascist when you justify your theory of dictatorial sovereignty in terms of the organic theory of the state and the concept of positive freedom. Also, to advocate a classless society is quite different from advocating marxism. You are only a marxist if you believe that the classless society will be brought about by the inexorable, materialistic, and dialectical movement of history. Marxists and fascists are in direct disagreement on these fundamental issues.

## DEMOCRACY

Democracy, like fascism, is a sociopolitical theory about the state, sovereignty, and the formal structure (i.e. government) through which sovereignty can best be effected. But unlike fascism, the basic concept of democracy is popular sovereignty. The democrat recognizes the need for more than individual sovereignty; the advantages of cooperative activity, and the impossibility of effective cooperative activity in a system of individual sovereignty, make that view unacceptable. At the same time, concerned with preserving as much individual freedom as possible, the democrat is very wary of the concentration of power that the rejection of individual sovereignty entails. For this reason he advocates popular rather than dictatorial sovereignty. Whatever abuses of individual freedom are possible under popular sovereignty, far more are possible under a dictatorial sovereignty.

In other words, although popular sovereignty is the basic concept of democracy, democratic theorists give up individual sovereignty begrudgingly. They believe that individual sovereignty is the ideal, but it is unworkable (see ch. 2, § Individual Sovereignty) primarily because genuine or effective freedom can only exist if a sovereign power works through the structure of government to protect that freedom. In other words, individual freedom is best served when the people is recognized as sovereign, although care must be taken to ensure that individual freedom is not eclipsed by the rule of the people.

Although all democrats agree on this much, there is much dispute among them on what individual freedom is and how much freedom is possible. Views range all the way from the libertarianism of Mill, which limits the scope of the people's authority to those acts which involve harm to others, to views that give almost absolute scope to the sovereignty of the people. An interesting form of this dispute involves negative freedom. This concept has two components. On the one hand, a person is free when he is externally unconstrained; on the other, when he has options open to him (i.e. the more options he has to choose from the freer he is). Some democrats focus on the first of these components. They believe that being left alone is what freedom is all about. Hence they feel that government should simply play the role of peace keeper. It should do nothing to enhance the lives of its members. It should prevent violence, theft, etc. and nothing else. It should keep its hands off the private lives of its citizens— politically, economically, and socially. In short, they believe that the government which governs least governs best.

In contrast to this view, other democrats focus on the option component of negative freedom. They say that the hands off policy does more harm than good. In the economic sphere it allows the rich to get richer and the poor to get poorer; in the political sphere the powerful get stronger and the powerless weaker; in the social sphere the depraved become even more debased. The only way to prevent this is for the government to play an active role in the lives of its people. In other words, the advantages of living in civil society must be made available to everyone, and so the government must guarantee that enough options are open to each member of society to ensure that he is free in substance as well as in form.

## The Common Good

Some thinkers attempt to reconcile popular sovereignty with individual freedom in terms of the common good. Here's their reasoning. Viewing both the state and the common good from the atomistic theory, most democrats believe that the way to achieve the common good is for each individual to pursue his own (private) good in a pluralistic society. In other words, just as the state is simply the sum total of the individuals who make it up, so the common good is simply the sum total of the good of the individuals who make up the group. Since each individual is in the best position to know what his own good is, individual good, and hence the common good, will be maximized if each individual primarily seeks to further his own good. Because some individuals may feel that their good requires the oppression of others, it is also important to ensure that the good of all individuals will be furthered to some extent. To this end pluralism, which requires compromise among competing interest groups for action, is introduced; it offers the best guarantee possible that everyone will get at least some of what he wants.[12]

In contrast to this approach, other democrats, albeit a minority, view the state and the common good from the organic theory and hence believe that everyone should pursue the common good rather than their private good. In other words, just as the state is more than the sum total of the individuals who make it up, so the good of the state (i.e. the common good) is more than the sum total of the good of the individuals who make up the state. Thus the furthering of individual good will not necessarily result in the furthering of the common good. Individuals must discover and pursue the common good rather than their own private good.

### *Relationships Between Organic and Atomistic Concepts of Common Good and Individual Freedom*

Any view that presupposes a common good in the organic sense requires that extensive limitations be placed upon the negative freedom of individuals who, for whatever reason, do not share the accepted conception of the common good. However this common good is determined—be it by the direct vote of the people or the insight of elected officials—it is the common good, and hence there should be at best little toleration of those who oppose it. For no group of people should have to tolerate for long individuals who seek to undermine the good of their group. The result is that individual freedom and minority rights play only a minor role in an organic conception of the common good. Dissidents should either be made to further the common good, or they should be excluded from the society by imprisonment or deportation.

The atomistic conception of the common good, on the other hand, supports rather than subverts the ideas of individual freedom and minority rights. In this view, every decrease in individual good results in a decrease in the common good. Moreover, because there is no conception of the common good other than that built from each individual's perception of his own good, there is no conception that individuals must be forced to accept. Each individual should do his own thing, promoting his own good (and the good of others if he cares to) as much as possible. Hence, individual freedom is the handmaiden of the common good.

Of course, only the extreme views are sketched here. In actuality, the line between popular sovereignty and individual freedom has been drawn in just about every conceivable way. But all theories of democracy maintain that popular sovereignty is a necessary means for protecting individual freedom, and attempt to reconcile the tension between the two.

### *Consent of the Governed*

A second element that all theories of democracy have in common is the idea of consent of the governed. Whereas the tension between popular sovereignty and individual freedom calls attention to the problem of minority rights and the tyranny of the majority, the idea of government by consent calls attention to something very different in nature. Popular sovereignty, the view that the people are sovereign, can only be effected through the formal structure of government. But how can this sovereignty be ensured once a government is created? What is to prevent the individuals who run that government from oppressing the people? Democrats answer, The government must be based upon the consent of the people. And this answer raises two further questions: (1) What constitutes consent? and (2) To what kinds of issues must this consent be given?

Consent of the governed is usually interpreted as majority rule. But not always. Sometimes a plurality is required, while in other cases a majority of two-thirds or even three-fourths is required. There are problems, however, in translating the idea of consent of the governed into a numerical formula for counting votes.

The first problem is, How can an individual be said to consent to an issue that he did not vote for, or that he voted against? For example, How can a black be said to consent to laws which discriminate against blacks when he expresses his opposition to such laws at every opportunity? Or how can the nonvoter be said to consent to anything? The problem is that if the nonvoter and the black do not consent, then it seems that they are not bound by the laws of their country; and if people are only bound by those things which they actively support or consent to, then all laws require unanimous consent, and we have a system of individual sovereignty rather than a system of popular sovereignty.

### Tacit Consent

The way to resolve this problem is to distinguish between two different senses of "government by consent." On the one hand, it may mean that each individual must consent to the enactment of each particular law or the outcome of each particular election. On the other, it may mean that each individual must consent to having a government, and that this consent entails abiding by majority rule.

If rather than consenting to the election of particular candidates or the enactment of particular laws, individuals consent to abide by majority rule,[13] they are committed to accept and abide by the will of the majority even when they do not share it. The assumption is that in a pluralistic society everyone will hold the majority view on some things and the minority on others. Only when everyone commits himself to abide by the will of the majority, even when he does not agree with it, can society exist. This idea is often expressed by the concept of "the loyal opposition"—the party out of power, although opposing some of the policies of those in power, supports the system by recognizing the right of those in power to implement their mandate.

Of course none of us has ever actually voted on the issue of whether or not we accept the idea of majority rule. But the point is that we all *tacitly* consent to it. By accepting the manifold benefits that society provides us—security, education, etc.—we tacitly consent to abide by the principle of majority rule; the only way to renounce this consent is to leave the country.[14]

### The Most Favored Candidate

But even if one accepts the idea of tacit consent, there is a second problem in translating the idea of consent of the governed into a numerical formula (e.g. majority rule) for counting votes. A vote for or against some individual, law, or policy does not take into account the intensity of the support or opposition for that individual, law, or policy. As a result, we can ask, Does the idea of majority rule (or any numerical formula) really capture the idea of government by consent?

Suppose that in an election between A and B, A received 55 percent of the votes, B 45 percent. A is clearly the winner of the election, but is he really the candidate most favored by the people? He may well be, but then again maybe he isn't. Suppose that most of the people who voted for A did not favor him by very much, but most of the people who voted for B favored him by a lot. In other words, suppose A was favored by 55 percent of the people, acceptable to another 5 percent, but strongly opposed by 40 percent. B, on the other hand, was favored by 45 percent of the people, acceptable to another 50 percent, and strongly opposed by only 5 percent. Although A is the winner on the basis of majority rule, there is a genuine question as to whether or not he is the most favored candidate. Given the intensity of the opposition, it may be more correct to say that B is the most favored candidate.[15]

It may well be that the intensity of one's support or opposition to a candidate, law, or policy is hard to quantify and even harder to take account of in a system of voting. It may also be that in actual fact, by sheer coincidence, the principle of majority rule does a very good job of approximating the outcome of votes based upon the intensity of support and opposition. But it is important to realize that the idea of consent of the governed is not identical with that of majority rule. Even though democratic thinkers tend to treat the idea of majority rule as a sacred cow, the basic notion in democracy is consent of the governed. Majority rule must be assessed in terms of how well or how poorly it reflects that consent.

But even if there is agreement on the method through which the consent of the people (i.e. the sovereign) is most accurately and effectively expressed, there is still the problem of determining what kinds of issues require this consent. Because the people are sovereign, but the country is run by the government, the problem of the relationship between the people and their government is crucial. Should the people merely elect the officials of the government or should they also consent to particular pieces of legislation and to particular policies?

### Consent to What?

To approach this question, one can ask, What kinds of decisions should be left to government officials and what kinds of decisions should be made directly by the people? On the other hand one can ask, When a government official makes a decision should he base it on his own perception of what is best, or should he do what the people think is best even if he thinks the people are wrong? The first question raises the dispute between direct (or participatory) democracy and representative democracy. The proponents of direct democracy (the democracy of ancient Athens that Plato argues against in *The Republic,* of the New England townhall meeting, and of the so-called New Left of the 1960s) insist that the people, by means of a direct vote, should decide all matters of legislation and policy. The only function of government officials is to carry out these laws and policies. Hence although government may have judicial and executive branches, there should be no legislative branch. All legislative matters must be taken directly to the people for their action. A direct democracy requires relatively small states, a method for quickly and accurately taking national referenda, or both.[16]

Representative democracy, on the other hand, is the view that legislation should be enacted by representatives. Rather than voting directly on matters of law and policy, the people should elect representatives who do this for them. Of course the people are still sovereign; if they do not like what their representatives do, they can vote them out of office. But the representatives, rather than the people themselves, are the legislators. Even within this framework, however, the same basic issue arises. Should a representative simply vote according to what his constituency wants, even if he believes it to be unwise, or should he vote according to what he thinks is best?

On the practical level, if a representative votes against the wishes of his constituency (especially on hot issues such as school integration, abortion, tax reform, etc.) there is a very good chance that he will not be reelected. In spite of this, however, some of the proponents of democracy still insist that legislators should vote according to what they think is best. Other democrats believe that the representative must truly represent his constituency by voting however he thinks they would vote, regardless of his own feelings. Those who take the latter view, although they support a representative structure of government, agree with the proponents of direct democracy—popular sovereignty requires that the consent of the people be expressed on all matters of government, not merely in the selection of officials. Those who believe that elected officials should follow their own consciences, take a different view. Popular sovereignty gives the people ultimate authority through the periodic chance to throw their elected officials out; it does not give the people a direct say in the particular decisions that every government must make.[17]

Let's imagine the dialectic of the dispute between these two camps. The proponents of the view that the people should be removed from legislative and policy decisions have doubts about the ability of the average citizen to intelligently make such decisions. Such a fear was at the heart of the decision to include the electoral college in the U.S. election system. Should the people make a bad choice for president, the electors (who would be chosen from among the elite) would be able to override them. In the legislative area, this kind of concern is still prevalent today. It is claimed that because legislative matters are so complicated it is impossible for the average citizen to make intelligent decisions about them. A team of experts is needed; this group does nothing but study and act on these matters, and the average citizen should be able to do no more than to elect these people.

The proponents of the other view—that the people should have a hand in legislative decisions either through direct referendums or by having elected representatives vote according to the will of their constituents—reject this claim. Although experts may be needed to research and lay out the issues on complicated matters, the people are as capable as the so-called experts to make the final decision. Of course a way must be found to keep the people fully informed; otherwise they could not make intelligent decisions. Given the judicious use of public and private television, this problem can easily be solved.

There are other points of disagreement between the two camps. The proponents of removing the people from legislative and policy decisions point out that people do not want to spend all their lives becoming informed about such issues; not only would they prefer to leave these decisions to others but, if these decisions were thrown upon them, they would not do the homework necessary for making them intelligently. Their opponents reply that these decisions are so important that, if the people were given a chance to make them, they would respond effectively.

The proponents, of keeping the people removed from legislation, speak of the need to make very quick decisions (especially when declaring war, responding to national disasters, averting economic catastrophe, and so on); not only does it take time to poll the people but their thinking tends to move much slower on such matters than does the thinking of elected officials. Opponents reply that the people can be polled quickly enough; maybe, if we moved a bit slower, we would not make the terrible kinds of mistakes that have been made in the past. And on it goes. . . .

### The Open Society

In addition to the problems of determining what constitutes consent and what things need to be consented to, there is also the more practical problem of ensuring that government by consent does not exist in form only. As we have seen many times before, having the proper form does not guarantee that the ideal is achieved. The mere fact that the people select their representatives, or even directly enact legislation, does not guarantee that they are really exercising their sovereignty. If they elect officials without knowing what their representatives believe, or if they enact laws that upon reflection they would not really favor, then their sovereignty has a hollow ring. If they accept whatever their elected officials do as right, and perfunctorily return those officials to office as a matter of course, then they are sovereign in name only.

Thus a society in which the people are sovereign in substance as well as in name requires more than the mere forms of democracy. It must be a society in which the people not only have the channels through which they can exercise their sovereignty, but also have the wherewithal to exercise it. The basic component of this wherewithal is an open society. In order to exercise their sovereignty intelligently, the people must have access to the information necessary to make intelligent decisions. At the same time they must have both the ability and the interest to assess critically this information and the conclusions others draw from it. To base decisions on false or inadequate information undercuts the very purpose of placing sovereignty in the hands of the people, whereas simply accepting the ideas of the leaders without drawing conclusions for oneself (even if the conclusions one comes to are the same as those drawn by the leaders) is in effect to give up one's sovereignty. Consent of the governed requires that the people be active participants in the decisions that face them, be it simply the election of officials or the passing of legislation.

This brings to the fore the question, Is genuine democracy (i.e. democracy in content as well as form) possible in the twentieth century? Two or three hundred years ago, this question revolved around the issue of whether the people as a whole had sufficient intelligence and restraint to govern themselves. The events of the last two hundred years require an unqualified affirmative answer to this question. The people may not always do the best thing with the greatest possible speed, but they do well enough with sufficient speed for democracies to succeed and flourish. But today the question, Is democracy possible? has a different meaning. The world has changed dramatically in the last several decades, and the basic challenge to democracy comes from a different source.

On the one hand, the world has become smaller. With the development of intercontinental systems of communications, transportation, and destruction, the fate of every nation in the world is inextricably tied to the fate of other nations. If dealings between nations are carried on in an open manner, this does not create any problems. But if the world situation requires secret acts (such as the United States' undeclared and unannounced war in Cambodia), and secret negotiations (such as the SALT talks), then it is impossible for the people to govern themselves, at least on these matters. Unrestricted classification of documents as "top secret," has been in vogue in the United States at least since the end of World War II. It poses a threat to democratic rule, because every document classified as "top secret" imposes a further restriction on the ability of the people to rule themselves. Although some classification of documents and other forms of secretive behavior may well be necessary on the international scene, there can be no doubt that this secretiveness has been almost as much abused as it has been used. Nevertheless the question remains, Is it possible for the people to have enough information about the affairs of state for them to make intelligent decisions, or does the state of the world require the secrecy that in effect transfers the sovereignty of the people to their rulers?

At the same time that the world has become smaller, it has also become larger. The population explosion of the last two hundred years has led to numbers of people previously undreamed of. To support this mass of people, many countries have developed highly integrated economies. Within these countries, actions taken in one area of the economy, even if rather small, can send shock waves throughout its entire system. The raising or lowering of taxes, the intervention or failure to intervene in a strike, the government's support of or failure to support education and health programs—all can have catastrophic effects. Moreover, the decision about what the government should do is as complicated and difficult as is the list of possible alternatives. Can these decisions be made by the people, or must they be made by experts? If they must be made by experts, then government by consent is no longer viable in the twentieth century.

These, then, are the basic problems facing democracy today. They are more fundamental than the more publicized challenges posed by the threat of nuclear destruction, the population explosion, and the energy crisis in the sense that their resolution will determine whether or not democracy can respond effectively to these challenges to life. In other words, the vitality of democracy depends upon the ability to shape the concepts of the common good, consent of the governed, and an open society so that they are relevant to the world in which we live. It is the urgency and importance of this task which makes the philosophical investigation of democracy in particular, and the issues of politics and society in general, such an important endeavor.

## NOTES

1. Some scholars maintain that the two are inconsistent—the early writings contain a youthful ebullience and foolishness that Marx later rejected. Others insist that, although the two are not inconsistent, the early writings reflect immature concerns which Marx later outgrew. And finally still others claim that not only are the early and later writings consistent, the later are the logical outgrowth of the early writings.

2. Karl Marx and Friedrich Engels, *The German Ideology,* ed. R. Pascal (New York: International Publishers, 1947), p. 14.

3. Ibid., p. 7.

4. See T. B. Bottomore, trans. and ed., *Karl Marx Early Writings* (New York: McGraw-Hill, 1964), pp. 120-39.

5. For a discussion of created needs see ch. 5, § Created Needs.

6. An interesting proposal for humanizing or de-alienating the divided work process is: Erich Fromm, *The Revolution of Hope* (New York: Harper & Row, 1968).

7. For example see Karl Marx and Frederick Engels, *The Communist Manifesto* (New York: International Publishers, 1948).

8. Georg Wilhelm Friedrich Hegel, *Encyclopedia of Philosophy*, trans. Gustav Emil Mueller (New York: Philosophical Library, 1959).

9. *Readings on Fascism and National Socialism*, ed. by members of the Department of Philosophy, University of Colorado (Chicago: Swallow Press, n.d.), p. 8.

10. Jean Jacques Rousseau, *The Social Contract*, rev. and ed. Charles Frankel (New York: Hafner Publishing Company, 1947), pp. 94-95.

11. *Readings on Fascism*, p. 35.

12. Another way of putting this point is that although utility (maximizing the common good) is the goal of society considerations of justice (making sure that the good of each individual is promoted) are also important.

13. Precisely what John Locke's formulation of the social contract says, see ch. 4, § Locke, All Agree to Abide by Majority Rule.

14. For a more complete development of this line of argument, see Plato's *Crito*.

15. For a more detailed discussion of this issue, see C. L. Dodgson (Lewis Carroll), *A Discussion of the Various Methods of Procedure in Conducting Elections* (Oxford: 1873). Partially reproduced in Thomas Schwartz, *Freedom and Authority* (Encino, California: Dickenson Publishing Company, 1973).

16. Because of modern technology, size is no longer an obstacle to direct democracy. It is now technically feasible to install a voting button in every home—the easiest way to do this would be to equip every TV set with such a button—and to have the votes instantly tabulated by a computer.

17. For a discussion of these and other theories of representation, see J. Roland Pennock and John W. Chapman, *Representation: Nomos X* (New York: Atherton Press, 1968).

# Glossary

The following terms are used recurrently and may prove troublesome. They appear in boldface type the first time they appear in the text.

**DESCRIPTIVE:** A *descriptive* statement provides information about an object by describing its properties. It does not evaluate that thing as good or bad, right or wrong, etc. Compare the *descriptive* statement, John has ten toes, brown hair, and a broken jaw, with the *normative* statement (see below), John is a good man.

**DIALECTICAL:** To say that philosophical investigation is *dialectical* means that it presents and evaluates reasons both for and against our beliefs. It precludes viewing any of these reasons (or beliefs) as "sacred cows" not to be questioned. All are to be critically examined, both in their own right and in relation to other beliefs. *Dialectic* is used in a special sense by Hegel and Marx. Hegel believes that the presentation and evaluation of reasons must proceed through the stages of thesis, antithesis, and synthesis. Marx takes this notion of dialectic and applies it to the movement of history rather than the reasoning process (see chapter 7, § The Dialectic).

**EMPIRICAL INVESTIGATION:** The testing of hypotheses about matters of fact through observation and experimentation. *Empirical investigation* reveals whether *descriptive* statements (see above) such as, It is raining, are true. *Empirical investigation* is the cornerstone of the *scientific method* (see below).

**EPISTEMOLOGY (EPISTEMOLOGICAL):** The study of the nature of knowledge. It seeks to answer the questions, What is knowledge? How does knowledge differ from mere belief? Is knowledge possible? What are the respective roles played by reason and the senses in the acquisition of knowledge? What can we have knowledge of? And so on.

**METAPHYSICS (METAPHYSICAL):** The study of what things really exist, and their true nature. *Metaphysics* studies those things whose existence and nature cannot be discovered through use of the *scientific method* (see below). It seeks to answer the questions, Is there a God? Do nonmaterial things such as souls or minds exist? Does every event have a cause? Is there such a thing as free will or free choice? And so on.

**NECESSARY CONDITION:** To say that A is a *necessary condition* of (or *necessary for*) B means that without A, B could not occur or exist. But it does *not* mean that A guarantees that B will occur or exist (see *sufficient condition*). For example, wings are a *necessary condition* of animal flight. This means that no animal can fly without wings. But it does *not* mean that all animals with wings can fly.

**NORMATIVE:** A *Normative* statement evaluates something as good or bad, right or wrong, and so on, by comparing it to a standard or norm. Compare the *normative* statement, John is a good man, with the *descriptive* statement (see above), John has ten toes.

SCIENTIFIC METHOD: A method for gathering information about the world. A problem is identified, related data gathered, a hypothesis formulated (usually on the basis of a scientific theory) to explain the data, and the hypothesis tested by *empirical investigation* (see above).

SPECIES: A subclass of a larger class. For example, a robin is a *species* of bird. Similarly, the question, What is social and political philosophy?, is a *species* of the question, What is philosophy?

SUFFICIENT CONDITION: To say that X is a *sufficient condition* of (or *sufficient for*) Y means that whenever X occurs or exists, Y must also. But it does *not* mean that Y cannot exist without X (see *necessary condition,* above). For example, making a killing in the stockmarket is a *sufficient condition* of being wealthy. This means that making a killing in the stockmarket guarantees you are wealthy. But it does *not* mean that if you do *not* make a killing in the stockmarket you cannot be wealthy. There are other ways of becoming wealthy (e.g., inheritance, theft, etc.).

# Suggestions for Further Reading

The following list of suggested readings is highly selective. Care has been taken to exclude from the list material too difficult for introductory level students. For a more extensive bibliography, see Thomas Schwartz, ed., *Freedom and Authority* (Encino, Calif.: Dickenson Publishing Company, 1973). Except for those items designated hard cover (HC), all entries on the list are available in paperback.

### Chapter 1. The Underlying Concepts

#### Introductions to Philosophy

Beardsley, Elizabeth L., and Beardsley, Monroe C. *Invitation to Philosophical Thinking*. New York: Harcourt Brace Jovanovich, Inc., 1972.
Wheatley, Jon. *Prolegomena to Philosophy*. Belmont, Calif.: Wadsworth Publishing Company, 1970.

#### Introductions to Social and Political Philosophy

Benn, S. I., and Peters, R. S. *The Principles of Political Thought*. New York: Free Press, 1965.
Feinberg, Joel. *Social Philosophy*. Englewood Cliffs, New Jersey: Prentice-Hall, 1973.

#### Collections of Readings

Olafson, Frederick A., ed. *Society, Law, and Morality*. Englewood Cliffs, New Jersey: Prentice-Hall, 1961. (HC)
Schwartz, Thomas, ed. *Freedom and Authority*. Encino, Calif.: Dickenson Publishing Company, 1973. (HC)

### Chapter 2: Sovereignty and the State

#### Dictatorial Sovereignty

Hobbes, Thomas. *Leviathan* Parts I and II. Indianapolis: Bobbs-Merrill, 1958.
Plato. *The Republic*. Translated by H.D.P. Lee. Baltimore: Penguin Books, 1955.

*Popular Sovereignty*

Locke, John. *The Second Treatise of Government.* Indianapolis: Bobbs-Merrill, 1952.
Rousseau, Jean Jacques. *The Social Contract.* Revised and edited by Charles Frankel. New York: Hafner Publishing Company, 1947.


*Individual Sovereignty*

Krimerman, Leonard I., and Perry, Lewis. *Patterns of Anarchy.* Garden City, New York: Doubleday, 1966.
Wolff, Robert Paul. *In Defense of Anarchism.* New York: Harper & Row, 1970.

### Chapter 3. Freedom

Dewey, Robert E., and Gould, James A., eds. *Freedom: Its History, Nature, and Varieties.* London: Collier-Macmillan Limited, 1970.
Skinner, B. F. *Beyond Freedom and Dignity.* New York: Alfred A. Knopf, 1971.


*The Metaphysical Problem*

Berofsky, Bernard, ed. *Free Will and Determinism.* New York: Harper & Row, 1966.


*The Sociopolitical Problem*

Berlin, Isaiah. *Four Essays on Liberty.* London: Oxford University Press, 1969.
MacCallum, Gerald C., Jr. "Negative and Positive Freedom." *The Philosophical Review* 76 (July 1967): 312-334.
Marcuse, Herbert. *An Essay on Liberation.* Boston: Beacon Press, 1969.

### Chapter 4. The Social Contract, the Rule of Law, and Natural Rights

*The Social Contract*

Hobbes, Thomas. *Leviathan* Parts I and II. Indianapolis: Bobbs-Merrill, 1958.
Locke, John. *The Second Treatise on Government.* Indianapolis: Bobbs-Merrill, 1952.
Rousseau, Jean Jacques. *The Social Contract.* Revised and edited by Charles Frankel. New York: Hafner Publishing Company, 1947.

### The Rule of Law

Fuller, Lon L. *The Morality of Law.* New Haven: Yale University Press, 1964.
Hart, H. L. A. *The Concept of Law.* Oxford: Clarendon Press, 1961. (HC)

### Natural Rights

Melden, A. I., ed. *Human Rights.* Belmont, Calif.: Wadsworth Publishing Company, 1970.

### Chapter 5. Utilitarianism and Justice

Frankena, William K. *Ethics.* 2d ed. Englewood Cliffs, New Jersey: Prentice-Hall, 1973.

### Utilitarianism

Smart, J. J. C., and Williams, Bernard. *Utilitarianism for and Against.* Cambridge: At the University Press, 1973.
Smith, James M., and Sosa, Ernest, eds. *Mill's Utilitarianism.* Belmont, Calif.: Wadsworth Publishing Company, 1969.

### Justice

Bedeau, Hugo A., ed. *Justice and Equality.* Englewood Cliffs, New Jersey: Prentice-Hall, 1971.
Perelman, Ch. *The Idea of Justice and the Problem of Argument.* Translated by John Petrie. London: Routledge & Kegan Paul, 1963. (HC)
Rawls, John. *A Theory of Justice.* Cambridge, Mass.: Harvard University Press, 1971.

### Chapter 6. Limitations on Sovereignty and Government

### The Nonintervention Principle

Mill, John Stuart. *On Liberty.* Edited by Currin V. Shields. Indianapolis: Bobbs-Merrill, 1956.
Wasserstrom, Richard A., ed. *Morality and the Law.* Belmont, Calif.: Wadsworth Publishing Company, 1971.

*Limitations on Government*

Connolly, William E., ed. *The Bias of Pluralism.* New York: Atherton Press, 1969.
Hamilton, Alexander; Jay, John; and Madison, James. *The Federalist.* New York: The Modern Library, n.d.
Pennock, J. Roland, and Chapman, John W. *Voluntary Associations: Nomos XI.* New York: Atherton Press, 1969. (HC)


*Chapter 7: Marxism (Communism), Fascism, and Democracy*


Cohen, Carl, ed. *Communism, Fascism, and Democracy.* 2d. ed. New York: Random House, 1972.


*Marxism (Communism)*

Bottomore, T. B., trans. and ed. *Karl Marx Early Writings.* New York: McGraw-Hill, 1964.
Dupré, Louis. *The Philosophical Foundations of Marxism.* New York: Harcourt, Brace Jovanovich, 1966.
Marx, Karl, and Engels, Frederick. *The Communist Manifesto.* New York: International Publishers, 1948.


*Fascism*

Palmieri, Mario. *The Philosophy of Fascism.* Chicago: The Dante Alighieri Society, 1936. (HC)
Members of the Department of Philosophy, University of Colorado, eds. *Readings on Fascism and National Socialism.* Chicago: Swallow Press, n.d.


*Democracy*

Dahl, Robert A. *A Preface to Democratic Theory.* Chicago: The University of Chicago Press, 1956.
Frankel, Charles. *The Democratic Prospect.* New York: Harper & Row, 1962.
Pennock, J. Roland, and Chapman, John W. *Representation: Nomos X.* New York: Atherton Press, 1968. (HC)

# Index